PLAYING THE JOB-FINDING GAME

A Rule Book for Ex-Offenders

PLAYING THE JOB-FINDING GAME

A Rule Book for Ex-Offenders

Terry Pile

PLAYING THE JOB-FINDING GAME:
A Rule Book for Ex-Offenders

Copyright © 2012 by Terry Pile

Cover Design by Jaime Patneaude, University Book Store Press
Interior Book Design by Anna Micklin, University Book Store Press

Published by University Book Store Press
4326 University Way NE
Seattle, WA 98105
www.ubookstore.com

ISBN 13 978-1-937358-04-4
ISBN 10 1-937358-04-6

Manufactured in the United States of America
First Edition

Dedicated to my students, who are my greatest source of knowledge for helping ex-offenders find employment

Thank you to
Carolyn Bledsoe, King County Jobs Initiative
and
Greg Hope and Sumonnat Puttavon,
Refugee Resettlement Office,
for the opportunity to work with the
ex-offender population

Additional thanks to Marci Hobbs, my editor, and
Carolyn Glassman and B. James Law, my readers

TABLE OF CONTENTS

INTRODUCTION

What Do I Know About Finding Jobs for Felons?

I teach ex-offenders how to find jobs. Most of my "students" have been incarcerated for drugs, assaults, theft or embezzlement. A few have been convicted for violent crimes or murder. These individuals are often a mixture of young, wiry white guys or well-built black men who played football or basketball during better days. There are always a few Hispanics, aging males and perhaps a woman or two among them. Occasionally, there is an individual who is well educated and worked in management; others never made it through high school, and their work history is scanty. A few wear their bizarre tattoos and gunshot scars proudly, sometimes pulling back a sleeve or lifting up a shirt to give the curious a better look. There is always one student with his head on the desk sleeping, another reading the Bible or a popular paperback. A few are sipping Mountain Dew and breaking into their cookies or Doritos, which have been packed in brown paper sacks and handed out by the work release officer. They are meant for lunch, which is still at least three hours away.

You can see the amusement on the students' faces when I walk into the room on the first day of class, dressed in my matching sweater set and wool slacks with a funky pin on my lapel -- a different one for each of the four days I will be teaching this group. What can this prissy, old squirt of a woman teach me about getting a job, they wonder? What does she know about street life, prison life -- or my life? I used to think they were right. What kind of credibility could I, a 60-something white woman from the suburbs whose greatest crime has been a speeding ticket, possibly have with this group?

But over the years, these students have taught me just as much about looking for work with criminal backgrounds as I have taught them about how to overcome this barrier and find employment. Based on their experiences and candor, I have been able to put together a vital and practical program to help them find employment, despite their past mistakes and transgressions. It has been a privilege for me to have these men and women open up about their lives and offer their insights into finding work in a marketplace that is highly competitive in the best of times. As my gift to them, I have packaged our collective wisdom and written this book, so that others, like you, who are looking for work after serving time, will know that support is out there. You are not alone.

About the Author

I am a career counselor, and this is my third career. I graduated from Indiana University in the '70s with Bachelor's and Master's degrees in education. After teaching elementary school for seven years, I took what I thought would be a temporary break from the classroom to work for a nonprofit agency. There, a 20-year career in public relations and marketing was born. I eventually worked as a senior account executive for an international marketing agency and, later, as the marketing director for a medical center. By the end of the 1990s, I was ready for a change and enrolled in the University of Washington career development certificate program. In 2000, I started a private career counseling practice called Career Advisors. Now, once a month I am back in the classroom -- teaching ex-offenders to market themselves to find employment through the King County Jobs Initiative.

Because of my background, I take a marketing-oriented approach to job finding. Throughout this book, you will see terms like *commercial* or *sales pitch* (also known as an "elevator speech"), *marketing materials* (job applications, resumes, cover letters, thank you notes) and *targets* (potential employers). You will learn how to do *market research*, prepare *key message points*, develop *marketing plans* and identify *strategies* to find employment. No company would consider selling a product without going through these paces.

King County Jobs Initiative Training Program

The King County Jobs Initiative (KCJI) is a nationally recognized program that helps ex-offenders prepare for, find and keep living wage jobs. The focus of KCJI is on providing job training in employment areas that have the most potential for wage growth. It also assists with job placement and supportive services to ensure the client's long-term success. Because of the success of KCJI, the program recently received the Washington state governor's Best Practices Award. I share a tiny part of that success. Before individuals can qualify for the KCJI program, they must attend my four-day workshop on preparing for employment. If they attend all four days, arrive on time, come prepared and complete the assigned work, they can enter the KCJI job training program.

Success Stories Gleaned from Others

Over the last six years, I have taught this workshop almost once a month and have come to know hundreds of ex-offenders, some with whom I am still in contact. Each time I teach this class, I glean a valuable tip, collect a few more stories or find a gem of a resource, and pass it along to the next group of students. By now, the class is rich in content, exercises and success stories, many of which are contained in this book. In some cases names and details have been changed slightly to protect individual identities.

How to Use This Book

So welcome to my workshop. Take off your coat and make yourself comfortable. Feel free to eat, drink or chew gum. We're all adults here. You're not in a classroom or in a prison. I am simply sharing my knowledge of how to overcome a criminal record to obtain employment. It is up to you to take as much as you want from this information and put it to good use. If you pay attention, complete the exercises and read the success stories along the way, you will be successful at finding employment -- just like others before you.

As you read this book, consider yourself the president/CEO of You, Inc. Like any successful business, you will want to market yourself in the work place with the same kind of careful preparation.

What the Symbols Mean

Quick Tip   **True Story**   **Exercise**   **Example**

EXERCISE

Before you begin, you may want to test your job-finding IQ. This will help you identify and focus on the areas in which you may be weak and will want to improve. After completing the book, come back to this page and retest yourself. I know you will be pleased with the results.

Test Your Job-finding I.Q.

1 – STRONGLY DISAGREE   5 – STRONGLY AGREE

	Before	After
1. I am clear on the type of career/job I want to pursue.	1 2 3 4 5	1 2 3 4 5
2. I have the knowledge and skills to pursue this career/job.	1 2 3 4 5	1 2 3 4 5
3. I have a resume that clearly shows, by examples, that I have the skills to perform in this particular field.	1 2 3 4 5	1 2 3 4 5
4. I know the best way to look for jobs.	1 2 3 4 5	1 2 3 4 5
5. I know which jobs are best suited for ex-offenders.	1 2 3 4 5	1 2 3 4 5
6. I know what to say when potential employers ask about my record.	1 2 3 4 5	1 2 3 4 5
7. I can articulate my major accomplishments.	1 2 3 4 5	1 2 3 4 5
8. I can develop a job referral network.	1 2 3 4 5	1 2 3 4 5
9. I know how to uncover job leads.	1 2 3 4 5	1 2 3 4 5

10. I have a list of at least 10 questions to ask in an   1 2 3 4 5   1 2 3 4 5
    interview.

11. I know how to respond when asked about salary.   1 2 3 4 5   1 2 3 4 5

12. I can answer commonly asked interview questions.   1 2 3 4 5   1 2 3 4 5

13. I know how to best follow up after a job interview.   1 2 3 4 5   1 2 3 4 5

14. I have developed positive mechanisms for   1 2 3 4 5   1 2 3 4 5
    handling rejection.

Which of the above job search skills are of most concern to you?

_____

_____

_____

_____

_____

_____

_____

CHAPTER 1: THE RULES OF THE GAME

Anyone who has ever looked for a job knows that employers don't always pick the most qualified or experienced job candidates. In fact, it is sometimes said that employers hire with their hearts and justify with their heads. All hiring decisions are based on some degree of subjectivity. This isn't necessarily a bad thing. For someone with a criminal record, sharing a love of motorcycles or rooting for the same football team as the hiring manager may be just the right move that gets him the job.

In reality, finding a job is like playing a game. Those who know the rules of the game, are strategic and can get into the mind (and heart) of the employer are the people who get hired. However, if you insist on taking the "what you see is what you get" or "I don't play games" approach, be prepared for a long job search. Being authentic gets you points with friends and relatives -- and employers -- once you are hired. However, for any job-seeker, with or without a criminal record, getting a foot in the door requires some degree of gamesmanship.

At this point in my workshop, someone will invariably blurt out, "So you are saying we should fake it to get a job?" No, definitely not. However, I do believe there are three important rules to follow if you want to win at the job-finding game and I will explain them in greater detail below. They are:

- **Rule #1: Think like an employer**
- **Rule #2: Mind your spin**
- **Rule #3: Stay focused**

Rule #1: Think Like An Employer

The first mistake most job candidates make is to focus on what they want in a job. I am not saying your employment needs and desires aren't important, but the reality is that the employer doesn't care. When an employer looks at your resume, he or she doesn't care if you want to work for "a dynamic organization that will allow me to use my skills and grow with the company." Instead, the individual is thinking, "Why should I hire this person? What value can she bring to my organization?" This is called the WIIFM factor -- "What's in it for me?"

As you prepare your resume and other job-finding materials, you will want to keep in mind, "What is in it for the employer to hire me?" To do that, you need to know what the employer is looking for. Below are the top 10 criteria most employers consider when they are contemplating hiring a job candidate

1. **Do you have the skills and qualifications to do the job?** Usually, employers can tell if the job candidate has the skills and qualifications for the job by looking at his or her resume. If they see a good match, they will request an interview. For example, if an employer is looking for a warehouse worker, he may want to see that the job candidate has had experience working in other warehouses, is forklift certified, and can operate a stacker and bar code reader. If he sees these skills on a resume (and spots no red flags like gaps in employment or multiple jobs in one year), the job candidate has a good chance of getting an interview.

Quick Tip

Don't expect an employer to believe you when you say you are dependable. Show him. If you have received an award or certificate for perfect attendance, show it during the interview.

2. **Are you dependable?** Employees who frequently come in late or call in sick cost the employer time and money -- time figuring out how to get the job done with fewer employees and money if they have to hire someone from a staffing agency to fill in. These employees don't remain in jobs very long. The job candidate who can convince the employer he or she can be counted on to show up every day and on time will move to the top of the list.

3. **Are you trustworthy?** Of course employers want to hire people they can trust, especially if there are large sums of money, expensive tools, machinery or technology involved. This is why most employers conduct background

checks. This is also where it gets tricky for the ex-offender. If you have broken the law in the past, how can the employer be assured you won't do it again? There are two good strategies you can use to convince an employer of your trustworthiness. First, you can remind the employer that you can be bonded through a federal or state bonding program specifically for ex-offenders. (See Appendix A) An employer will be more inclined to risk hiring an ex-offender knowing the employee is bondable. A second strategy to overcome the trust factor is to have three to five positive references lined up. If others can vouch for your trustworthiness, the employer may be willing to give you a chance. (References are discussed in Chapter IV.)

True Story

Randy spent seven years in prison playing pinochle. When he got out, he had very little work experience to speak of. He decided to volunteer for a nonprofit organization that dismantled computers and recycled the parts. Randy learned the job quickly and was good at it. He was frequently left on his own to manage the shop. He had earned the volunteer coordinator's trust and was considered to be someone who could be depended upon to work independently and get the job done. Not only did Randy gain a great reference, but this experience is one he will want to share with an employer in an interview.

4. How quickly can you learn the job? Training a new employee can be costly. Therefore, most employers want to hire individuals with previous experience, which can be frustrating for someone with very little work history. How can you get experience if no one will hire you unless you have experience? This is where likability becomes particularly important. If an employer likes you, she may be inclined to hire and train you, despite your lack of experience.

5. How much supervision will you require? Can you work independently? Again, it comes down to time and money. Most employers don't have the time or the resources to micromanage their employees. They want independent thinkers and doers, people they can leave on their own and know the job will get done.

6. Are you a self-starter? Do you take initiative? Most employers like people who take on tasks without being told. Employees who are proactive and take initiative are often promoted to greater responsibility. If you are the kind of person who stocks empty shelves or picks up trash from the parking lot without being told, you probably have the initiative an employer is looking for.

7. How well can you solve problems? Employers like people who can independently solve problems and don't need constant input. Whether you are dealing with people, numbers or things, demonstrating that you are good at solving problems will earn you points with an employer. Start writing down some of the problems you have solved on the job, at school or in prison. These may be "stories" you will want to relate to the employer during an interview.

8. Can you work well with others and are you pleasant to work with? This is one of the most important factors an employer considers when making a hiring decision. He wants someone who can get along with staff, clients and vendors. Employers want low-maintenance employees. It is easier to train someone to use a milling machine than it is to train that person to be positive and cooperative. No matter how technically capable you may be, if you create conflict and negativity, no one will want you on the team.

9. Can I afford you? Whether you are buying a new appliance or hiring a contractor, when all things are equal, cost is often the tie-breaker. An employer may like you, but if you are asking for more money than he or she can pay, the job will go to your competitor. How do you know what is a fair wage to ask for? How do you avoid revealing past income on a job application or in an interview? (This is discussed in Chapter IV.)

10. How long will you stay in the job? High employee turnover is costly and time-consuming. Therefore, employers want to know that the potential new hire will stick around. Questions such as, "What are your career goals?" or "Where do you hope to be three years from now?" are really probes to determine if you are looking for longevity with a company or will bale out for any job that pays a few cents more. Since you don't have a crystal ball, you can honestly assure the employer that you plan to stick around and grow with the company.

EXERCISE

How well do you think like an employer? Test your knowledge with this multiple choice quiz.

1. The job candidate has several misspelled and crossed-out words on the job application. You think ...
    a. Anyone can make a mistake.
    b. The person must have forgotten to bring his dictionary along.
    c. This person is clearly uneducated or careless and lacks pride in his work.

2. You ask the job candidate what he knows about your company. He says that he didn't have time to do the research. You think ...
    a. This must be someone with a busy social life.
    b. That's ok. I don't need a researcher, I need a carpenter.
    c. This guy just wants a job and doesn't care who he works for.

3. After the interview, you receive a thank you note from the job candidate.
You think ...

>   a. This guy is a real goodie-two-shoes.
>   b. Only management types write thank you notes.
>   c. This person appears very professional and must really want to work for me.

If you chose "C" for each of your answers, congratulations. You are thinking like an employer.

Quick Tip:

Words like "felon" or "convict" are highly charged words and should be avoided. Instead, use terms like "ex-offender," "served some time," "broke the law" or "a person with a record." These words are not as loaded and are more acceptable to the general public. At some point in your job search, you will have to discuss your conviction. Think about how you will spin your story. You can't lie or sugar coat it, but neither do you have to ignite the employer's imagination with highly charged words. If you were convicted of assault, you might be able to say you "got into a fight." If you went to jail for manslaughter, it may have been an accidental shooting. Describe your offense directly and briefly, then bridge to the positive. You can read some sample scripts in Chapter VI. Then prepare your own script and test it out on a few trusted friends. You should never be taken by surprise when someone asks you about your conviction. This should be a carefully crafted and well-rehearsed speech.

Rule #2: Mind Your Spin

During one workshop, I asked a student, Pete, if he would volunteer to talk about his conviction. "Sure," he said. "I got busted for drug trafficking." My mind immediately conjured up an image of Pete driving across the Mexican border in the dark of night with bricks of heroin stashed in the spare tire of his Honda. To me, someone with little experience with the law, the words *drug trafficking* sounded like a very serious offense. After a little bit of coaching, I again asked Pete to tell me about his conviction. He responded, "I made a very bad choice and got involved with recreational drugs." This time the image in my mind is of me, sharing a joint with my friends back in college and almost getting caught by the cops. Now Pete doesn't seem like such a criminal after all, and I can empathize with his unfortunate incarceration.

Some career counselors will tell job candidates to take control of the interview. I think this is bad advice. However, you can -- and should -- take control of the information you provide to people and the choice of words you use. In the world of marketing and public relations, we call this "spin." Some examples of spin are calling a used car a "previously owned vehicle" or referring to a garbage man as a "sanitation engineer." As with Pete, using loaded words like *drug trafficking* creates all kinds of images in an employer's mind. If you want to play the game and win, choose your words carefully and think of the impact they will have on the listener.

EXERCISE

Learning how to spin responses to difficult questions takes some practice. Select the best spin for each of the questions below.

1. Were you ever fired from a job?
   a. Yes, I had a co-worker who didn't like me and lied about me to the boss.
   b. Yes, I was hired for a job in which, as it turned out, my skills weren't a good fit for the work required.
   c. Yes, at my last job I came in late a few times so they fired me.

2. What is the worst mistake you have ever made?
    a. Robbing a bank.
    b. Not finishing high school.
    c. Getting into a fight a week before my parole hearing.

3. Tell about a time you had a conflict with your boss.
    a. I had a boss who didn't pay me because he didn't like the work I
       did, so I walked off the job.
    b. I generally get along well with my bosses. I figure you can always
       learn something new even if you might not always agree.
    c. I had a boss who was a micromanager. I hate being micromanaged.

If you selected "B" for each of the three questions, you are well on your way to
becoming a "spinmeister."

Rule #3: Stay Focused

On the first day of a recent job-finding workshop, I asked the students what kind of jobs they were looking for. Ray answered, "I'll take any job. I just want to start earning some money to support my family." Anita said, "I am looking for work as a receptionist. I worked for an auto dealer in the past and I was really good at answering phones and helping customers."

Which of these students will have an easier time finding employment? If you said, Anita, you are correct. Anita knows exactly what she wants to do and why she is good at it. Because she has a clear goal, I know exactly where to help her start looking for jobs and how to package -- or spin -- her marketing materials (resume and cover letter). With Ray, I am not at all sure where to begin helping him. If he is unclear about the kind of job he wants, how can he expect the employer to know he is the right person for the job?

When most ex-offenders have served their time, they are eager to get back into the work force. They will take just about any job to earn a paycheck. But if you think like an employer, you understand that most hiring managers want to hire people who want to work for their companies and show enthusiasm for the jobs they will be doing. An employer knows that if it is "just a job," you probably won't give it your best effort or be in the position for very long.

Job searchers who are focused on a specific job function or occupation are likely to find employment they are well-suited for and obtain it more quickly than someone who is applying for any job for which he or she is remotely qualified. This doesn't mean you must pick one job option above all others. If you are skilled in carpentry, delivery driving and data entry, prioritize your choices and focus on one occupation at a time. You will want to prepare a sales pitch, resume and list of potential employers related to each occupation you are pursuing. Not only is this a more efficient approach to finding a job, but it is also much more effective.

True Story:

When Mark got out of prison, he was eager to find employment. Prior to his incarceration, he worked as a cook in a family restaurant and in a warehouse for a furniture manufacturer. He put together a resume that reflected both of his career experiences -- food service and warehouse work. In the skills section of his resume he listed his ability to operate a forklift, ship and receive freight, track inventory, create new menu items, practice food safety and fry, poach and roast foods. These are impressive skills, but Mark's phone was not ringing with interview requests. He was not thinking like an employer. When employers saw Mark's resume their first thoughts were, "This person just wants a job. He doesn't care if he is flipping hamburgers or moving widgets. I want someone who is really committed to the work he does."

After taking my job readiness workshop, Mark decided he needed two resumes, one focused on food service and one for warehouse work. On the food service resume, he included only the food service skills he acquired, expanded on his experience in the restaurant and minimized his warehouse work. He reversed this strategy on the warehouse resume. After Mark focused each resume for the specific occupation and made the appropriate adjustments, his phone started ringing.

CHAPTER II: RULES FOR GETTING INTO SHAPE

Whether you are getting ready for the game of basketball, football, chess or job-finding, it is important to be prepared physically and mentally for peak performance. This chapter highlights two factors to help you get into shape for the job-finding game:

- Overcoming barriers to employment
- Setting goals for success

Overcoming Barriers to Employment

Almost every person looking for a job has to leap some hurdle to obtain employment. It could be age, a gap in work history or poor interviewing skills. For the ex-offender, having a criminal record sets the bar even higher, but the bar isn't insurmountable. Based on feedback from the students in my workshops, I've outlined below the most common obstacles to employment ex-offenders face and suggestions for breaking them down.

A criminal record

Identify felony-friendly industries.

Although it is difficult to find felon-friendly employers, some industries and companies tend be more lenient than others when it comes to hiring people with criminal records. These industries include manufacturing, construction trades, environmental services, transportation and hospitality. It is important to know which occupations are generally off limits to ex-offenders. Law enforcement, education and most health care jobs fit into this category. Of course the type of conviction will also impact the kind of work you can get. If you were convicted for reckless endangerment with a vehicle, you probably shouldn't look for jobs that require you to drive. On the other hand, this may be of little concern to an employer looking for a tool and die maker. Refer to the General Job-finding resources in Appendix A to help you research industries, occupations and employers prior to starting your job search.

Connect with social service agencies.

Some community agencies have special funding to assist ex-offenders in finding employment. These agencies are generally partnered with employers that have agreed to hire ex-offenders. Take advantage of the support they provide. If you maintain a lone ranger mentality when it comes to the job search, you will easily get discouraged. Check with the one-stop career centers in your state to find out if there are special programs that provide employment assistance to ex-offenders. (www.careeronestop.org) Also contact Goodwill Industries, the Salvation Army and faith-based organizations in your area. Many sponsor programs to get ex-offenders back into the work force.

Remind employers about tax credits and bonding programs.

Employers may not be aware that they can get tax credits for hiring someone convicted of a felony. The Work Opportunity Tax Credit allows employers a maximum credit of $2,400 for hiring an ex-offender within a year of conviction or release from prison (www.doleta.gov or 800-318-6022). The Federal Bonding Program guarantees the honesty of at-risk job applicants for six months by offering employers fidelity bonds to cover damage and theft from $5,000 to $25,000. There is no cost to the employer, and the process is very simple. However, you must have the job offer to be eligible for the bonding program (www.bond4jobs.com or 877-872-5627). Federal and state tax credits and bonding assurance are incentives you will want to mention to convince an employer to hire you.

Volunteer in your community.

At the mention of volunteer work, many students cringe and say, "I need a pay check. I can't afford to work for free." This is a short-sighted view of volunteering. By devoting a couple of hours to volunteer work once a week or a couple times a month, you are demonstrating your work ethic, giving back to the community and developing a network of supporters who will want to help you find a job or possibly hire you. Pick your volunteer work strategically. If you want a job in the trades, volunteer for Habitat for Humanity. This organization builds low-income housing using volunteer power and it doesn't do background checks. Looking for warehouse work? Volunteer at a food bank. Want a job as a delivery driver? Volunteer to drive the activity van for your church or a senior center. Volunteer Match is a great online resource for matching people with volunteer opportunities compatible with their interests. (www.volunteermatch.org)

Lack of experience or poor work history

Study successful resumes.

There are many ways to "spin" your resume and other marketing materials to camouflage a lackluster work history. Chapter IV and the examples in Appendix B will help you develop your marketing materials in a way that focuses on your positive qualities and achievements, while avoiding the weaknesses.

Include prison jobs on your resume.

Don't discount the work you did in prison. If you worked in the kitchen or laundry, performed janitorial services or worked on a road crew, you acquired skills that can be transferred to work outside of prison.

Consider temporary self-employment.

If you don't have much work experience, create it. Call yourself a freelance handyman and start mowing lawns or cleaning garages for your neighbors. Offer to help family and friends with odd jobs. You can find pick-up work on community job boards or Craigslist under the heading "Gigs." Grab any job you can find to build up your work experience -- and your resume.

Quick Tip:

When including an "inside job" on your resume, there is no need to mention that it was performed in prison. State your job title, "Kitchen Worker," and list the employer as, "The Department of Justice" or "The State of Nevada." Most likely, the reader will assume you were a paid employee of this institution.

Volunteer in your community.

Look for volunteer work that will help you acquire new skills and expand your work experience. Many nonprofit organizations need help with clerical work, facility maintenance and event planning. Depending on your conviction, you may be able to find a volunteer job working with at-risk youth or coaching a little league team. Is there a skill you want to enhance? There is probably an organization out there that would love to give you that opportunity. (www.volunteermatch.org)

Lack of education

Get a GED.

An overwhelming number of ex-offenders have less than a high school education. In today's marketplace, it is highly unusual for an employer not to require a high school diploma or GED. You can find out about GED programs by contacting your local community college.

Quick Tip

"Once you replace negative thoughts with positive ones, you'll start having positive results."

-- Willie Nelson

Find a job training program or apprenticeship.

Many of the social services agencies previously mentioned can direct you to job training programs and apprenticeships appropriate for ex-offenders. The more education and skills you acquire, the more marketable you will become.

Improve your computer skills.

Today's job searcher is at a distinct disadvantage if he or she doesn't have adequate computer skills. Increasingly, employers are posting jobs and requesting applications online. Although this isn't necessarily the best way to look for a job (more about this later), having basic computer skills for job searching is a must to maximize your options. Your one-stop career center, local library and many service organizations, such as Goodwill Industries and the Salvation Army, offer computer classes at no or low cost.

Volunteer in your community.

Is this starting to sound like a broken record? I can't emphasize enough the value of volunteering to enhance your education and develop your work ethic.

Lack of confidence or negative attitude

Power of positive thinking.

Not a single individual who has walked into my office has been excited about looking for a job. Writing resumes, finding job vacancies, getting hiring managers to return phone calls and handling rejection are generally activities most people want to avoid. However, if you perceive the job search as an opportunity to create a new future for yourself, it can be an exciting journey, full of hope and promise. Using positive self-talk is critical when your self-esteem is ebbing. When you wake up in the morning, spend a few minutes visualizing what your day will be like and the successes you hope to realize. Get in the habit of keeping a journal. At the end of each day, write down one positive thing that happened.

Create a network of support.

Surround yourself with people who want to see you succeed. These people may not always be family and friends. Everyone involved in a job search needs a fan club to cheer him or her on. This might mean joining a club, attending a place of worship or, yes, volunteering. You want people on your team who can boost your spirits when you are down and give you the pep talk you need to keep going. Consider case managers, counselors, teachers, fellow students, family, friends and neighbors. Dabble in the social media to find groups of like-minded, positive people who can support you in finding a job. Avoid friends who may be bad influences and limit your contact with negative people.

True Story:

When I met Ralph, he had just started a work release program after more than a decade of incarceration. "I have so much catching up to do," he told me. "I just enjoy talking to people and living life." Ralph knew things weren't going to be easy with his skimpy work history and criminal record. But he clearly appreciated what he did have -- his new freedom. I knew that Ralph's positive outlook would get him over any employment barrier he faced.

Celebrate small victories.

Don't dive into a job search expecting immediate results. Celebrate your accomplishments each step of the way. Identifying the jobs you want, creating a resume, identifying potential employers and getting invited to interviews are all small steps to getting employment, and each of these acts should be cause for celebration. Don't beat yourself up if you only sent out three resumes last week. Celebrate that you made three employer contacts!

Volunteer in your community.

I'm saying it again! Volunteering not only improves the lives of others, but it also provides intrinsic reward. We feel good about ourselves when others have benefited from our actions. If you need a boost in your morale, volunteer to help a family member, neighbor or community agency. Your efforts will be rewarded.

Setting Goals for Success

A research study conducted by Dr. Gail Matthews of Dominican University showed that individuals who wrote down their goals and shared them with friends were, on average, 33 percent more successful in achieving them than those who simply formulated goals. Goal advocates often remind others of Bill Clinton's written commitment, made in his teens, to become president of the United States. Whether this is an urban legend or not, it appears that writing down goals and letting others know about them creates a sense of direction and accountability. There are a few important points to remember when developing your goals:

> **Quick Tip**
>
> "If you want to lift yourself up, lift up someone else."
> -- Booker T. Washington

- **Short-term versus long-term.** Short-term goals can generally be accomplished within one year. They are stepping stones to reaching your long-term goal or vision, which could take several years to accomplish. For example, learning how to use a computer for job-finding is a short-term goal that will help you reach your longer-term goal of finding a job.

- **Include an action plan.** Once you state what you want to accomplish, write down steps for how you want to do it. If your goal is to improve your computer skills for job-finding, your plan of action might be to take a class at the local one-stop career center, pay a friend to teach you or learn on your own by working through a self-help book.

- **Keep goals realistic.** You want goals that make you stretch, but you also want them to be achievable. If your goals are too lofty or unrealistic, you may become discouraged. Learning how to use a computer for job finding is a reasonable goal to helping you find employment. But if you are expecting this new skill to land you a six-figure job, you may have set unrealistic expectations.

- **Set a deadline.** Attach a deadline for completing your goals so the process doesn't drag on indefinitely. You may want to complete that computer class next week, next month or by the end of the summer, but an end should be in sight.

Keep your list of goals readily available and review it often. Limit yourself to two or three short-term goals and one long-term goal. There is something very satisfying about achieving a goal, crossing it off your list and replacing it with a new one. Now let's practice goal setting.

Quick Tip:

"Give me a stock clerk with a goal and I'll give you a man who will make history. Give me a man with no goals and I'll give you a stock clerk."

-- J.C. Penny

EXERCISE
Practice writing goals.

Create a goal for overcoming an employment barrier. List the outcome you hope to achieve, action steps for how you plan to do it and a deadline for accomplishing your goal.

Goal or achievement:_____
_____
_____

Action steps:
1. _____
2._____
3._____

Deadline for completion:_____

Create a goal for learning a new skill. List the skill you hope to acquire, action steps for how you plan to do it and a deadline for accomplishing your goal.

Goal or achievement:_____
_____
_____

Action steps:
1. _____
2._____
3._____

Deadline for completion:_____

CHAPTER III: RULES FOR WARMING UP

The very first time I taught the job-finding workshop to ex-offenders, 12 men were in the class and they could easily have been mistaken for offensive linemen. I would be lying if I said I wasn't totally intimidated. One man with a shaved head, Mark, must have weighed close to 300 pounds and was covered with tattoos. When I asked him about the skills he had, he laughed sarcastically and said, "Skills? I don't have any skills. I haven't worked for 10 years, and before that my job was selling drugs."

After further questioning, albeit gently, I discovered Mark had worked in the prison kitchen, where he used math to adjust recipes to serve several hundred people. He had knowledge about safe food handling and was responsible for tracking and ordering food inventory. He had acquired knife skills and could roast, fry and bake. His prison job had given him enough experience to put together a more than acceptable food service resume. Once Mark realized that he was in fact "marketable," his attitude changed from one of skepticism to enthusiasm.

In this chapter we will cover

- Identifying your marketable skills
- Creating your stories
- Matching your skills to the job

Identifying Your Marketable Skills

I said earlier that the best person for the job isn't always the one to get hired. The person who understands the skills he or she has to offer and how to market them has the best chance of landing a job. So let's talk about how to identify your marketable skills.

Skills that can be taught are often referred to as hard skills. You can be taught to operate a forklift, take inventory, network a computer or run a cash register. These skills are learned on the job, in a school or training program, or they can be self-taught. You can demonstrate that you have these skills by the certifications you've obtained, the types of jobs you've held or through performance tests.

Soft skills, on the other hand, are much harder to learn and to demonstrate. Soft skills are innate abilities or personality traits, such as being a team player, using good judgment, being dependable and working independently. It is much harder to determine if someone has these soft skills, and they are also harder to teach. This is where stories come in handy. If an employer says she is looking for someone who is a "quick learner," you can describe a time you were able to learn a new skill quickly to get a job done. We will discuss how to use stories later in this chapter.

True Story:

"When I was helping my uncle in his auto body shop," said Steve, "he wanted me to enter two months-worth of service orders into a database. I had never used Microsoft Excel before, but I was able to have the office manager show me a few quick tips and provide me with an instruction manual. Before the end of the day, I had input a backlog of over 200 orders. My uncle thought it would take me at least two days and was scrambling to find me more work."

See how powerful a story can be? Steve's story is a great example of how he is quick to learn and apply new skills. As you begin identifying your hard and soft skills, think of examples you can provide an employer that are proof you really do possess those skills.

EXERCISE
Assessing Your Skills (Hard Skills)

Highlight the skills you enjoy doing and do well. Then write examples next to these skills to prove you can do them.

Communication Skills:
Influence/persuade_____
Interpret/translate_____
Motivate others_____
Negotiate_____
Read documents_____
Sell/promote_____
Speak/present publicly_____
Write reports_____
Mediate conflict_____

Management Skills:
Supervise/lead people_____
Analyze information_____
Assign/delegate work_____
Evaluate performance_____
Fire/hire _____
Prioritize work_____
Advise/consult

Creative Skills:
Act/perform_____
Design _____
Invent_____
Paint_____
Use humor_____
Write creatively_____
Build or make things_____
Come up with creative ideas_____
Improve processes_____

Computer Skills:
Keyboarding_____
Programming_____
Networking_____
Troubleshooting_____
Debugging_____
Data entry_____
End user support_____

Administrative Skills:
Plan/organize_____
Coordinate_____
Collect_____
Copy_____
Dispatch/distribute_____
Purchase/order_____
Type/word process_____

Report_____
Research_____
Schedule_____

Manual Skills:
Cut_____
Bind/fasten_____
Drive_____
Move/lift_____
Load/unload_____
Ship/receive_____
Drill_____
Deliver_____
Inspect_____
Install_____
Operate_____
Assemble_____
Set up/adjust_____
Repair_____

Financial Skills:
Budget_____
Gather data_____
Analyze numbers_____
Track expenses_____
Tabulate _____
Pay bills_____
Prepare invoices_____
Reduce costs_____

Teaching Skills:
Train/teach_____
Coach/mentor_____
Explain_____
Facilitate_____
Inform_____
Demonstrate_____
Guide_____

Helping Skills:
Care for_____
Protect_____
Nurture_____
Help others_____
Provide_____

Other skills:
_____

EXERCISE
Assessing Your Personal Traits (Soft Skills)

Identify the personal traits you possess. Give examples of why you believe you have these traits.

Accurate_____

Ambitious_____

Articulate_____

Assertive/bold_____

Business-minded_____

Calm_____

Capable_____

Careful_____

Caring_____

Cheerful_____

Clever_____

Confident_____

Considerate_____

Cooperative_____

Creative_____

Curious_____

Dependable/reliable_____

Detail-oriented_____

Determined_____

Easygoing_____

Energetic_____

Focused_____

Friendly_____

Healthy_____

Helpful_____

Honest_____

Imaginative_____

Independent_____

Industrious/hard working_____

Intelligent_____

Intuitive_____

Loyal_____

Mature_____

Methodical_____

Observant_____

Open-minded_____

Optimistic_____

Outgoing_____

Patient_____

Persuasive_____

Pragmatic/realistic_____

Punctual_____

Quick learner_____

Quiet_____

Resourceful_____

Responsible_____

Self-disciplined_____

Sensitive_____

Serious_____

Sincere_____

Sociable_____

Tactful_____

Teachable_____

Thoughtful_____

Trusting_____

Trustworthy_____

Understanding_____

Versatile_____

Wise_____

Creating Your Stories

Now that you have identified some of your skills and personal traits, let's look more closely at those examples and expand on them. Think about something you have done in your work, volunteer or prison life that you enjoyed doing, did well and that really made you feel proud. Write out your "proud moment" using the Background, Actions, Results (B.A.R.) format below. Be sure to give each story a one-or two-word name. Here are some suggestions to help you think of stories. An example is provided below:

- ☐ Helping a customer or co-worker
- ☐ Finding a problem and fixing it
- ☐ Winning an award for good work
- ☐ Showing you are a team player
- ☐ Teaching someone a new skill
- ☐ Finding a faster way to do a job

- ☐ Making a mistake and fixing it
- ☐ Planning a special event or meeting
- ☐ Making/building something from scratch
- ☐ Showing you are an honest person
- ☐ Doing a job without being asked (initiative)
- ☐ Improving a system or procedure

EXAMPLE

Story Name: Buttermilk Pancakes

Background: What was the situation? What obstacles or challenges did you face?

While working in an institutional (prison) kitchen, it was my responsibility to make the buttermilk pancakes on Sunday morning. After making a few batches, I realized that we were going to run out of buttermilk.

Actions: What steps did you take to achieve your desired goals?

Since our facility had a library, I quickly went over and referenced a couple of cookbooks. Sometimes they offer suggestions for substitutions. I discovered I could make my own buttermilk by adding a tablespoon of white vinegar to

---

one cup of regular milk. I knew we had white vinegar because we also use it for cleaning.

I added 20 tablespoons of vinegar to 20 cups of milk. That translated to 2.5 cups of vinegar for 5 quarts of milk. Then I let it sit for five minutes and proceeded to finish making breakfast.

Results: What was the outcome of your efforts? Can you quantify the results?

As a result, several hundred diners got buttermilk pancakes and were spared a big disappointment. I also learned a valuable lesson -- to check the ingredients the night before so I don't run out. It has never happened again.

List the skills, knowledge, abilities and personal traits required to perform the above task.

Resourceful -- knew where to find helpful information
Accountable -- accepted that a mistake was made and learned from it
Creative problem solving -- figured out a way to deliver on an expectation
Customer service -- went the extra mile to avoid disappointing the customer
Math and cooking skills -- adjusted recipe for a large group

EXERCISE

Prepare at least five stories you could use in an interview. Use the B.A.R format.

#1. Story Name: _____

Background: What was the situation? What obstacles or challenges did you face?

Actions: What steps did you take to achieve your desired goals?

Results: What was the outcome of your efforts? Can you quantify the results?

List the skills, knowledge, abilities and personal traits required to perform the above task.

#2. Story Name: _____

Background: What was the situation? What obstacles or challenges did you face?

Actions: What steps did you take to achieve your desired goals?

Results: What was the outcome of your efforts? Can you quantify the results?

List the skills, knowledge, abilities and personal traits required to perform the above task.

#3. Story Name: _____

Background: What was the situation? What obstacles or challenges did you face?

Actions: What steps did you take to achieve your desired goals?

Results: What was the outcome of your efforts? Can you quantify the results?

List the skills, knowledge, abilities and personal traits required to perform the above task.

#4. Story Name: _____

Background: What was the situation? What obstacles or challenges did you face?

Actions: What steps did you take to achieve your desired goals?

Results: What was the outcome of your efforts? Can you quantify the results?

List the skills, knowledge, abilities and personal traits required to perform the above task.

#5. Story Name: _____

Background: What was the situation? What obstacles or challenges did you face?

Actions: What steps did you take to achieve your desired goals?

Results: What was the outcome of your efforts? Can you quantify the results?

List the skills, knowledge, abilities and personal traits required to perform the above task.

EXERCISE

Once you have completed the skills checklist and your stories, look for patterns. Are there skills and personality traits that keep appearing? These are called your transferable skills -- skills you can transport from one job to another. Consider the skills from the checklist and your stories. Write down what you consider your six strongest hard and soft skills/personality traits.

Hard skills: Soft skills:

1._____   1._____

2._____   2._____

3._____   3._____

4._____   4._____

5._____   5._____

6._____   6._____

Matching Your Skills to the Job

You have identified your skills and personal traits and provided examples or stories to back up your claims. Next, consider how these skills can be transferred to jobs you may want in the future. Each occupation has its own particular set of skills. Painters must be able to prepare surfaces and choose the appropriate paint or finishes. They need to be able to remove old paint by stripping, sanding, wire brushing or abrasive blasting. In addition, a painter needs to know how to fill holes and cracks, work with scaffolding and dispose of paints and thinners in a safe manner.

These are the hard skills of the job. Painters should also possess personal qualities, such as being precise, thorough, safety-conscious and neat. If you are considering a job as a painter, you may not have all the hard skills the employer is looking for, but you can learn those. If you can convince the employer that you have the soft skills or personal traits required of a painter, he or she may be willing to hire and train you.

The Occupational Outlook Handbook (www.bls.gov/oco) will provide you with job descriptions of the most common occupations, as well as job projections, educational requirements, salaries and much more. You can find this resource online or locate a hard copy in your local library. Read through a variety of job descriptions. Once you have found a few that you think would be a good match with your skills set, write down the hard and soft skills required for that particular occupation.

EXAMPLE

Hazmat Technician	Roofer	Retail clerk
- Abates lead, asbestos, mold and mildew	- Performs heavy lifting	- Waits on customers
- Uses and maintain personal protective equipment	- Works outside in all types of weather	- Deals with angry/difficult customers
- Uses hand/power tools	- Works with tar, asphalt, metals and shingles	- Operates a cash register
- Follows directions	- Works in high places, on scaffolds and ladders	- Answers phones
- Works well in teams	- Is safety conscious	- Stocks shelves
- Is safety conscious	- Works independently	- Is friendly and helpful
		- Takes initiative

EXERCISE

List the occupations you are considering and some of the hard and soft skills involved. Many of these skills should match the ones you have listed in the previous exercise.

Occupation: Skills:	Occupation: Skills:	Occupation: Skills:

True Story

Prior to his incarceration, Jackson worked at a financial call center. When he got out of prison, he responded to a staffing agency job posting for a position requiring similar financial knowledge at a bank call center. The recruiter liked Jackson's resume, called him and sent him to interview with the employer. Although Jackson explained that he had a felony, the recruiter encouraged him to do the interview anyway. Jackson got a second interview and was close to a job offer before his parole officer intervened. Jackson had been convicted for robbing a bank and this job was off limits according to the conditions of his parole. If Jackson had transferred his call center skills to a different industry, it is very likely he would have been gainfully employed.

CHAPTER IV
RULES FOR FINE-TUNING YOUR EQUIPMENT

Any competitor playing to win should make sure that his equipment is in tiptop condition. It is no different when you are playing the job-finding game. Your marketing "equipment" should be in tiptop condition in order to sell your benefits to the employer. These materials include:

- Commercial or sales pitch
- Business cards
- Job applications
- Resumes
- Cover letters
- Thank you notes
- Skills portfolio

Creating Your Commercial or Sales Pitch

Tell me about yourself. Take advantage of this invitation to let people know what kind of job you are looking for and the value or "perk" you can offer. Some people call it a sales pitch, others an elevator speech (meaning you should be able to sell your benefits in the time it takes to ride an elevator). Regardless of what you call it, this is a commercial about YOU. It shouldn't be your life story. It should focus on the job you want in a simple and memorable way. The goal is to be clear in communicating your career objective so that others will be able to help you. You are creating a sales force to promote YOU. Your commercial is spoken and should include the following:

- **P**osition or job focus
- **E**ducation and/or **E**xperience
- **R**ecommendations -- What others say about you
- **K**now-how -- Why you will be good at this job

Eventually, you will formalize your commercial. It will become the summary statement at the top of your resume. You will also use it in interviews, making it more specific to each job for which you are interviewing. Remember to keep your commercial brief, but informative. You don't want to memorize it, but if you follow the PERK format, you should have no trouble remembering your key points. Here are some sample commercials:

EXAMPLES

Warehouse worker

(P) I am looking for warehouse work. **(E)** My experience includes working at Pete's Quality Moving Company. I recently earned my forklift certification at Central Community College and can safely operate a pallet jack and shrink wrapping equipment. I am very accurate at taking orders, doing inventory and maintaining a safe and clean work area. **(R)** My last supervisor described me as someone who is very positive and can always be depended on to get the job done right. **(K)** This job sounds like a good fit for me because it will allow me to work on a team and use a variety of skills I already have, so I can hit the ground running.

Customer service specialist

(P) I enjoy working with people and am looking for a job as a receptionist. **(E)** One of my favorite jobs was at an advertising agency, where I answered up to six phone lines. Another job I enjoyed was solving customer problems at an auto dealership. I was recently certified in Microsoft Office Suite through the King County Jobs Initiative Program. I keyboard up to 50 words a minute and am extremely organized and accurate. **(R)** My coworkers frequently comment that I am dependable and personable. They know they can always count on me to get the job done -- with a smile. **(K)** I am looking for a position where providing excellent customer service is the number one priority, and I believe your company shares this goal.

Hazardous materials removal worker

(P) I am a hazmat technician. **(E)** I have had more than 240 hours of training and am licensed to perform lead, asbestos and mold abatement. I have also worked in construction, which gives me an advantage in knowing how things are constructed and how to operate heavy equipment. **(R)** My instructors have told me I am a quick learner, conscientious and have excellent manual dexterity. **(K)** My work is very rewarding in that I am doing something good for the environment and protecting people from harmful substances. I am looking for an employer that does abatement work and I understand your company has a very good reputation in the industry. That's the kind of company I am looking for.

Quick Tip:

It is often easier to talk about yourself when you do it through the voice of other people. Phrases such as "My supervisors have said..." or "My customers have told me..." lend an air of credibility to your commercial and it doesn't feel as if you are bragging.

EXERCISE

Write your commercial here. You may want to use this template to get yourself started, but don't be afraid to get creative. Keep your commercial to under 150 words so it will be easy to remember.

(Position) I am looking for a job as a _____

(Education/Experience) My related training includes_____

_____

Some of the jobs I have had were _____

_____

_____

_____

(Recommendations) People (bosses, co-workers, customers) have told me I am

_____

_____

(Know-how) I know I will be good at this job because _____

_____

Preparing Your Business Cards

The business card is your most cost-effective form of self-promotion because it is easy to carry with you and easy for people to keep on file. If you want to be a successful networker, don't leave home without it. The cost for business cards is wide ranging, but for most people, using an online service that offers free business cards (with the service's advertising on the back) is adequate. Vista Print (www.visitaprint.com) offers 200 free business cards plus the cost of shipping (about $6). If you don't have a credit card, you can pay by check. There are dozens of designs to choose from, and for a few dollars more you can remove the company ad and customize your card. It is also easy to create your own cards using software such as Microsoft Publisher. The business card stock you buy should feel substantial, and your card, if homemade, should look professional.

What do you put on the business card? That depends on your career focus. If you aren't sure what you want to do next or the jobs you want are very diverse, you can simply include your contact information. If you are buying "free" business cards, you may want to have a different card for each occupation. You may also want to include a tagline or slogan that represents who you are and what you stand for. In advertising, we call this your brand. Study the sample business cards below to help you decide the type of content you want to include on your card.

 EXAMPLE

Benjamin "Bugsy" Siegel
HANDYMAN

On-call ~ On-time ~ On-budget

718-228-1906
bugsysiegel@hotmail.com

P.O. Box 620, Brooklyn, NY 11218

Blanche Barrow
b.barrow1@yahoo.com

General bookkeeping
Data entry
Transcription
405.101.1911 ~ Garvin, OK 74736

Butch Cassidy

Cassidybutch@gmail.com
435-212-1866

Exceeding expectations -- always!

Filling Out Job Applications

My advice when it comes to filling out job applications is DON'T. It is much more effective to use a resume, get the interview and then fill out the job application as a formality. Job applications are designed to screen people out, especially if you are an ex-offender. Put yourself in the place of a human resources specialist with 200 applications on her desk. You will start by eliminating the ones that aren't signed, indicate criminal records, don't include a high school diploma or GED, or are riddled with misspellings. Now you have narrowed your selection to a few dozen. There are many other ways a job application can trip you up. Here are a few ways to avoid this:

Appearance. If you are submitting a hard copy of your application, make sure there are no coffee stains, torn corners and crossed-out words. First impressions count on paper as well as in person. It is best to do a practice application and then copy the information to a clean application, keeping the original for your file. If you walk into a company to fill out a job application, make sure you bring a black or blue pen, a master application with employment dates, addresses and phone numbers, correction fluid to cover errors and a dictionary.

Personal information. It is illegal for employers to ask your age, marital status and ethnicity on a job application. However, they often like to gather that data to be eligible for tax credits. Generally, this information is collected separately from your job application and considered optional. Fill it out if you think it is to your advantage to do so; otherwise, avoid it.

The Social Security number is always requested on a job application, but employers don't need this information unless you are a job finalist. Then they will want to do a background check. Because identify theft is common today, most employers make this information optional until they need it. In the blank space that asks for your Social Security number, write in "Available at interview." This lets the reader know that you haven't skipped the request; you are just waiting until the interview to provide this information. Because of the cost, most employers don't do background checks until after they have interviewed a candidate and are pretty sure they

Quick Tip:

Avoid filling out electronic job applications. They aren't as flexible as the printed form. If you don't have a choice, try to find the name of the hiring manager at your target company and send her a copy of your resume. Online job applications are generally a waste of time. In Chapter V, I'll discuss more effective strategies for getting your foot in the door.

want to make an offer. This allows you to warn a potential employer about your past in advance, so there are no surprises when the background check comes back with a report of your past conviction(s).

Have you ever been convicted of a crime? This is the question all ex-offenders dread. It is definitely meant to screen out law-breakers or at least raise a red flag. Meeting the employer and getting him or her to like you prior to filling out a job application can render this question moot. Some job applications will add a time limit for convictions of seven or 10 years. Others will distinguish between a felony and a misdemeanor. Read the question carefully. Then you have two options. (Lying is not one of them.) You can leave the question blank and explain your record in the interview, or you can respond with one of the following phrases:

- Yes, will explain at interview
- Yes, have met all legal obligations
- Yes, prior to ... (add a date if it has been more than 10 years)

Do not go into a lengthy explanation. It won't help and can only hurt your cause.

How many employers do I list? Most employers want to see your last 10 years of employment in reverse chronological order (newest to oldest). I recommend inserting the word "Relevant" on the application and listing the jobs that are similar to the position you are applying for. You can also insert the words "Other Employment" and list unrelated jobs on just one line if you have worked for prestigious companies or want the employer to know you have a work history that extends beyond 10 years.

Reasons for leaving your last job. Keep this answer brief and general. Avoid using terms like "more money," or "personality conflict." Acceptable answers are "New opportunity," "Relocated," "Career Change," or "Retraining." If you were doing seasonal or contract work, were laid off or the company closed, it is OK to say so. Unless the application asks you explicitly if you were ever fired from a job, use the term "not a good fit."

The salary question. Depending on how you answer this question, it may automatically eliminate your chance for an interview or get you a job offer substantially below market rate. Therefore, it is best to avoid numbers. If the application asks for the salary desired, your response should be "open" or "negotiable." However, job applications often ask you for your wage at each job. If you had jobs that paid wages higher than the employer is offering and you state those salaries, the employer will probably remove your application from consideration -- assuming you cost too much. If you were making prison wages or minimum wage, you don't want to state that either or there is a chance you will be "low-balled" when negotiating compensation. The safest response is to put "market rate" in the salary section for each job. You are saying you made the going rate for a particular job at a specific time and geographic location. Let the employer figure out the rest.

References. If you are concerned about putting the name of a former super-visor on your job application, put "Contact Human Resources" instead and provide the general business phone number. Many companies will only allow the human resources staff to provide references, and the information they give out is minimal. Make sure you have three strong advocates to list in the reference section of the job application. These can be former bosses, teachers, clergy, co-workers, vendors, staff you supervised and customers. If you have been volunteering, ask the volunteer coordinator you work with for a refer-ence. Always get permission from your references first and inform them if they are about to get called. It is OK to coach your references by giving them the job description, a copy of your resume and filling them in on the skills and attributes the employer is looking for.

Developing Your Resume.

If you give your resume to 10 different people, you will get back 10 different opinions. Even professional career counselors don't agree on style, format and resume rules. The most important thing about a resume is that you should be comfortable with it. You are the one who must defend it, so you should be the final decision-maker as to what goes on your resume. Most career counselors will agree a successful resume should adhere to the following three rules:

- **A resume must be accurate.** You can't add jobs you have never had, education you never completed or employers you never worked for. Lying on a resume will just get you into trouble down the road. Don't do it.

- **A resume must be relevant.** In the information age, there is no such thing as a general or one-size-fits-all resume. Your resume must reflect the specific job you are seeking. You may need three or four resumes if the jobs you want have different skill sets. Even if you have a

Quick Tip:

Avoid asking the Human Resources person for a pen when you walk in to fill out a job application. This will make you look unprepared and unprofessional. Dress the part when you are applying for a job. The minute you walk into a company, people are unconsciously forming their impressions of you.

very good "carpenter resume," you still may want to tailor it for each carpenter job you apply for.

- **A resume must show your value.** One common mistake people make is to write their job descriptions, but omit their job accomplishments. Be sure to show on your resume the value you brought to your job as well as the tasks you performed. Did you make or save your employer money? Reduce delivery time or errors? Improve productivity? Try to quantify these results using numbers or percentages.

True Story:

When Alison was preparing her resume for an office position, one of the skills she listed for her job in a real estate office was "answered phones." When I did a little probing I found out that Alison "answered six phone lines for an office of 20 real estate agents. "Answered phones" tells us what Alison did. However the second statement tells us that Alison can multi-task, handle phone technology and work in a high-volume setting. This second statement shows the value Alison can bring to the job. It is a much more powerful way to demonstrate her skills on paper.

Remember, think like the employer when you are writing your resume and show what is in it for her to hire you.

Now that you know the three universal rules to resume writing, read below the most typically asked questions regarding this marketing tool:

Chronological or skills-based resume? A chronological resume focuses on your work history, starting with your most recent job and working back. A skills-based or functional resume highlights your skills first, then mentions your work history toward the end of the resume. With a functional resume, it is more difficult to determine when and where you held each job. Individuals who have recently been released from prison are often advised to write functional resumes because it is easier to hide gaps in work history, i.e., prison time. Unfortunately, when hiring managers see a functional resume, their first thought is, "What is this job candidate hiding?"

The best use of a functional resume is in cases whereby your jobs have been in the same profession. If you have always been a welder and you plan on continuing welding, a functional resume is appropriate. Instead of listing the same skills over and over, you only have to list the skills once and then indicate the companies you worked for.

What are "key words?" When playing the job-finding game in a world driven by technology, there is a good chance no human being will ever see, touch, or read your resume if it doesn't include "key words." Key words are generally the hard and soft skills and qualifications associated with the position. Computer software is designed to scan resumes and search for key words and phrases to determine which resumes are a good match for the criteria the hiring manager is looking for. If the computer likes your resume, there is a good chance it will get read by a real live person. If the reader sees the value you can bring to her company, there is a great chance you will be invited in for an interview. Some key words for a construction foreman, for example, include: project management, supervised crews and sub-contractors, building codes, plumbing/electrical/HVAC/carpentry.

How long should my resume be and how far back should I go?
Today, there is no hard and fast rule as to resume length. Generally, employers want to see the last 10 years of your work history. My rule of thumb: If you don't have a lot of experience or if you are changing careers, stick to one page. If you have supervisory experience and a rich work history, don't cheat yourself by trying to cram it all to one page -- go to two.

One of the biggest mistakes job searchers make is to advertise their years of experience on the resume. For example, "Twenty years experience as an auto mechanic." If you are thinking like an employer, 20 years will sound expensive. Some people call this age discrimination. I call it experience discrimination or the overqualified syndrome. It just stands to reason that a job candidate with 20 years of experience will want more money than someone with 10. If an employer is looking for someone with 5+ years of experience, and you have 25, simply state that you have solid or extensive experience in the field. Wait until you get the interview to convince the employer that your "extensive experience" can work to his advantage.

EXERCISE

Take a look at the two job postings below and underline the key words for each job. Include the exact title of the position you are applying for.

Warehouse Worker Needed
Warehouse worker needed for second shift. Must be a certified forklift operator and be able to lift up to 50 lbs. Experienced in shipping and receiving domestically and internationally. We offer excellent benefits. Contact Lisa at 206-987-6543.

Kitchen Help Wanted
Food service worker needed in busy family restaurant. Looking for friendly and self-motivated individuals. Must have food handler's license. Experience with prepping and plating desired. Dishwashing and light janitorial experience required. Contact Oliver Popkin at www.olpop.com.

Compare the words you underlined with the key words here:

Warehouse Worker: Warehouse worker, second shift, certified forklift operator, lift 50 lbs., shipping, receiving, domestically, internationally

Kitchen Help: Food service worker, friendly, self-motivated, food handler's license; prepping, plating, dishwashing, light janitorial

Additional resume do's and don'ts

RESUME DO'S:

- Use standard white or cream paper -- colored or textured paper doesn't scan well in a computer.
- Use short, concise sentences or sentence fragments -- every word on a resume should be important. Take out pronouns (I, me) and unnecessary words such as "Responsible for handling cash of $1,000." Just say "Handled $1,000+ in cash."
- Put the most important information at the top of the page -- key words should go at the top of the resume in a section called a Summary of Qualifications.
- List volunteer work, professional/trade memberships, certifications and licenses, continuing education and awards.
- Be consistent in formatting and leave plenty of "white space" for easy reading.
- Include your name and page number if you use a second page; don't use the back of a page, it may not get noticed or scanned.
- Make sure your e-mail address is on your resume and your full name is included. John.paul. sellen@gmail.com is a more professional e-mail than love2fish@gmail.com and will keep your name in front of the recruiters.
- Proofread, proofread, proofread!

RESUME DON'TS:

- Misrepresent yourself or give false information.
- Use complete sentences or pronouns (I, me, our).
- Indicate that you have been incarcerated or give a reason for leaving a job.
- Include personal information or hobbies (unless relevant).
- Use jargon, slang or acronyms.
- Include salary information or references (including the statement "References Available Upon Request." This is assumed.)
- Use fancy fonts or type smaller than 10 point -- type without serifs, such as Arial and Verdana are good type fonts to use.
- Try to cram everything onto one page.
- Forget to proofread.

The anatomy of a resume

Header: It should include your name, address, phone number and e-mail address. Make sure your e-mail address is your name, not a clever moniker.

Objective: This is the professional focus of your resume. If you are applying for a specific job, the objective should match the title of the job you are applying for. If you are a customer service clerk, and the employer is hiring for customer care representatives, this is the job objective on your resume. The objective is one part of your resume you will be frequently changing.

Summary of Qualifications: This is your commercial put into writing. It should include the key words of the job description as well as the attributes you want to sell to the employer. Don't be afraid to use the employer's exact language. Remember, a computer is reading your resume and may not be able to interpret *handle money* if it is looking for *cashiering*. It is best to put key words into a list format so you can easily change them depending on the job description.

Work Experience: Employment should be listed in reverse chronological order with the most recent job listed first. However, here is where you may make exceptions, especially if a previous job is more relevant to the position you are applying for. In the resumes to follow, the work experience has been divided into two categories: Relevant Experience and Other Experience. This makes it possible to take similar jobs and group them together. You can also take the dates off of Other Experience if it is to your advantage. Work experience should include the following:

- Name of company, city, state
- Job title
- Beginning and ending dates
- Job responsibilities
- Job accomplishments -- statements that show your value

Education: Most career counselors will recommend you leave dates of education off your resume if it goes back more than five years. A resume reader should not be able to figure out how old you are by looking at your education. Be sure to include licenses, certificates and continuing education classes, and include dates if they are recent. Employers look favorably on job candidates who keep their skills current.

Awards: If you received a perfect attendance award, employee of the month award or a special commendation, include it. Even if you don't feel it is significant, others felt strongly enough to recognize you, so take credit for it.

Memberships: Union and professional memberships should be listed. Also list memberships in service groups, such as Kiwanis, Rotary or Toastmasters, past and present. Avoid mentioning specific religions or political and controversial groups such as the National Rifle Associaiton or Planned Parenthood. Resume readers bring their biases into their decision-making, whether it is conscious or not.

Foreign languages: If you are fluent in a language other than English, indicate this on your resume as employers may see it as a benefit.

Community involvement: Most employers like to see that job candidates have a life outside of work and a social consciousness. Volunteering is a great resume enhancer.

True Story:

Vernon worked as a cook on a research vessel more than 20 years ago. He really liked that job and wanted to apply for jobs as a cook on a cruise line or fishing boat. He didn't want the employer to know how long ago his last job as a cook was. After listing two of his most recent jobs working in a laundry, along with a refresher class he took in the culinary arts, Vernon added a section to his resume called Previous Experience. In this section, he listed his job as a cook on a research vessel, but omitted dates. It told the resume reader that he had experience, but not how dated the experience was.

Quick Tip:

One of the first things a resume reader looks at is dates to determine gaps in employment or multiple jobs in a short period of time (which indicates the candidate is a job hopper). De-emphasize dates by putting them at the right side of your resume and do not highlight. Also think about how dates can work for or against you. If you started a job in November 2010 and left the job in March 2011, you were only in the job about four months. By leaving off the months and just putting years (2010-2011), the reader may assume you have been in the job at least a full year, if not longer. However, if using the month and year works to your advantage, do so. If you started a job in January 2009 and left in December 2010, you want the employer to know you were in the position almost two years.

Study the resumes in this chapter. At first glance, you will probably be unaware that these individuals have criminal records. In these examples, jobs in which the state is the employer are the jobs that were performed while incarcerated. In some cases, the individual may have worked for a contractor of the state. It is legitimate to use the state contractor's name as the employer. You can find more resources and resume examples in Appendix A and Appendix B.

EXAMPLE
Chronological resume in 10 pt Arial type

CLYDE BARROW
1909 Chestnut Street, Telico, TX 75152
942-523-1934 ~ clyde.barrows@gmail.com

OBJECTIVE: Customer Service Representative

SUMMARY OF QUALIFICATIONS:
Energetic and hard working professional with excellent customer service experience and a strong work ethic. Worked in fast food, grocery and service industries. Skills include:
Handling money/cashiering
Taking inventory and stocking shelves
Solving customer problems
Performing light janitorial duties
Skilled at Word, Excel, PowerPoint and PhotoShop
Considered dependable, friendly and willing to pitch in when there's work to be done.

RELEVANT WORK EXPERIENCE:
State of Texas*, Huntsville, TX   2009 - 2011
Library Clerk
- Checked out books and shelved returned books for 20,000 volume library
- Offered reading recommendations to patrons, providing superior customer service
- Repaired damaged book covers as needed
- Maintained accurate records in library database; used Excel spreadsheets

Albertsons, Houston, TX   2008 - 2009
Courtesy Clerk
- Bagged groceries for customers, stocked shelves, performed janitorial tasks and other duties as assigned
- Set up program with local food bank, which accepted expired canned goods from store
- Substituted for other baggers on short notice
- Volunteered for special assignments and additional work hours

McDonalds, Wako, TX   2004 - 2006
Cashier
Served as a cashier at the customer service counter and drive-through window. Prepared drinks and ice cream cones, as well as other food items. Performed basic janitorial tasks
- Operated cash register and made change with high degree of accuracy
- Independently resolved issues with unhappy customers
- Stayed calm and performed well during "rush hours"

OTHER WORK EXPERIENCE:
Worked in yard care for a local landscaping company and as a bus boy for Denny's. **

EDUCATION:
- Currently taking business courses at Telico Community College, Telico, TX
- GED, Telico High School, Telico, TX

Note: * Held job while incarcerated. ** Reader may assume jobs were held between 2006-2008

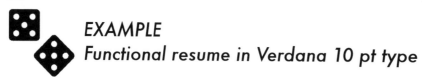

EXAMPLE
Functional resume in Verdana 10 pt type

Bonnie E. Parker

1920 Dallas Way, Rowena, TX

942-523-1934 ~ bonnie.e.parker@hotmail.com

FOOD SERVICE
Cook ~ Waitress ~ Hostess

Creative and energetic food service worker with experience in a variety of capacities in fast food and casual dining restaurants. Enjoy working in teams to create a positive dining experience for customers that will ensure repeat business. Areas of expertise include:

- Worked in kitchen, prepping and plating food; handled up to 250 meals per shift
- Created menu items and nightly specials, many by popular request
- Maintained a safe and clean work environment; performed light janitorial tasks
- Demonstrated safe food handling knowledge and excellent knife skills
- Skilled at broiling, frying, grilling, baking and barbequing; specialties include Italian, Cuban and American cuisines
- Supervised and trained up to six kitchen staff members
- Took reservations, greeted guests and waited on tables as necessary
- Checked food and supply deliveries against invoices to ensure accuracy of orders
- Considered to be friendly, hard working and a solid team player; dependable and self-motivated with strong work ethic

RELEVANT EXPERIENCE

Caterer, **Self-employed***, Rowena, TX - (2010 - present)
Line Cook, **World's Best Bar-b-q,** Houston, TX (2004 - 2006)
Wait Staff, **Quinton Family Restaurant**, Hillsboro, TX (2002 - 2004)

OTHER EXPERIENCE

Custodian, **Cleaning Services of America****, Jefferson, IN (2007 - 2010)

EDUCATION

- General Education Diploma, Rowena, TX
- Texas state food handlers license

COMMUNITY INVOLVMENT

Volunteer, Southwest Harvest Food Bank, food packer
Volunteer, Terre Haute Mission, serving meals to the homeless population

Note: * Cooked for family/friends after release; ** Held job while incarcerated.

Writing Cover Letters

The cover letter is a letter of introduction and is customized for the specific job you are applying for. Some employers do not want to receive cover letters, particularly if they are large employers receiving thousands of resumes. Others welcome the cover letter. They know many people hire professionals to write resumes, but most people write their own cover letters. This gives the employer insight into how well you communicate and how much you know about his company. Try to include a cover letter whenever possible. It is one more opportunity to link your skills, knowledge and experience to the job requirements. Below are cover letter suggestions and cautions:

Quick Tip

Avoid putting personal information, such as hobbies and interests, on your application. You never know how it will be perceived. You may think race car driving and bungee jumping are cool sports, but an employer sees them as liabilities that will impact the company's insurance rates.

COVER LETTER DO'S:

- Let the reader know exactly which job you are applying for and how you found out about it, i.e., on the company Web site, from a friend.
- Make sure your commercial is included within the body of the letter.
- Highlight a few accomplishments that are directly related to the job; don't be afraid to repeat what you have in your resume, although you might change the wording a bit.
- Let the reader know why you are interested in the company and how you can add value to the position.
- Check for spelling and grammatical errors -- then check again.

COVER LETTER DON'TS:

- Make your cover letter longer than one page. Do break up long paragraphs by using bullets.
- Address the letter "Dear Sir." Try to find a name or just put "Hiring Manager."
- Use the word "I" too much. Do vary the way you begin each sentence.
- Forget to include key contact information, like phone and address; put this in the header matching the style of your resume.
- Use abbreviations. Do spell out words.
- Forget to enclose your resume or sample work if you say you are enclosing them.
- Use tiny or hard-to-read fonts.

What to include in the cover letter:

- A header with your contact information
- Name of a contact person if you can find it
- Title of job you are applying for and job number if included
- Where you found out about the job
- Why you are interested in this company
- Why you are a good match for the job (link the requirements with your qualifications. Try to use as many key words from the ad or posting as possible.)

Quick Tip

If you are sending your resume to an employer online, include your cover letter within the body of the email prior to attaching your resume. Employers are more likely to open resume attachments, but seldom take the time to open cover letters that have been attached.

EXAMPLE: Cover letter Verdana 10 pt type
(Use as a letter or put in an email)

Alphonse Capone

312.117.1899 ~ al.capone@yahoo.com

1934 Cicero, Chicago, IL 47758

February 1, 2012

Att: Donald Hatchback, Recruiter
    Big Rigs Trucking Company

Re: Maintenance Mechanic #BG445

Dear Mr. Hatchback:
This is in response to your ad for a Maintenance Mechanic, #BG445, posted on your company Web site. I was pleased to see that Big Rigs has an open position that is a good fit with my skills and experience. Having recently relocated, I am looking for an employer with your reputation for service and safety.* Attached is my resume. Highlights of my qualifications include:

- Solid experience as a Maintenance Mechanic with the Eight Wheeler Company. While there, I maintained and repaired electronic motors and gasoline engines on a fleet of 50 trucks and heavy construction machinery.**

- Possess excellent mechanical skills and a good ability to find parts for the best price/quality. I saved my last employer $25 per wrench through my negotiations with a local supplier. ***

- Proven customer service skills, having received an Employee of the Month award for providing outstanding customer service.

My employers have described me as dependable, good natured and collaborative.**** I look forward to discussing how these qualities fit in at Big Rigs Trucking Company. Thank you for your consideration.

Sincerely,

Al Capone

Notes:
* Tell the employer why you want to work for him or her.
** Use language from the advertised position and show scope of work.
*** Offer a good example of the value you can bring to the employer.
**** Use "third party testimonials" or speak from another person's voice paraphrasing what others have (or might say) about you.

EXAMPLE: Qualification cover letter - Arial 10 pt type (This cover letter compares qualifications with job criteria. Good to use if the job is almost a perfect fit.)

JOHN H. DILLINGER
299.622.1903 ~ J.H.DILLINGER@GMAIL.COM
722 Corson Street, Indianapolis, IN

February 4, 2012

Lisa Plumber
Big Box Stores
2345 Safety Street
Anywhere, WA 98765

Dear Ms. Plumber:
This is in response to the ad on Craigslist for a Warehouse Worker for Big Box Stores. Attached is my resume. I am a good fit for this position for the following reasons:

You Require:	My Qualifications:*
• Experience shipping/receiving	• Solid experience shipping and receiving domestically and internationally, including ground, air and ocean
• Certified fork lift operator	• Worked more than 3 years as a certified fork lift operator; also operate hand/ power tools, pallet jacks and other heavy equipment
• Lift 50 lbs	• Maintain a regular fitness regimen and can bench press up to 300 lbs.
• Flexible hours	• Willing to work evenings, weekends and holidays

In addition, my employers have described me as a skilled problem solver and collaborative team member. I believe my experience and qualifications will enable me to jump right in and get the job done.**

Thank you for considering me for this position. From what I have read about Big Box Stores, I know you are growing and I would like to be a part of that expansion. *** I look forward to meeting with you to discuss in greater detail how I can contribute to Big Box Stores.

Sincerely,

John H. Dillinger

Notes:
* Always indicate that you have more than the job is asking for.
** Indicate that the employer will have to do very little training.
*** Show you have done some research on the company. You aren't looking for any old job.

Following Up to Set Yourself Apart from the Competition

How many of you send a thank you note to the hiring manager after an interview?

When I ask this question in my workshop, maybe one or two hands are raised. Many job seekers, especially in the trades, do not send thank you notes, which is exactly why you should. Having talked to hiring managers about thank you notes, I got responses similar to this one:

> "In the old days, people would send thank you notes after an interview. But it is very rare to get them today. Occasionally we get a thank you note from a job candidate, and it makes a definite impression."

The thank you note will set you apart from your competition. It is an additional opportunity to sell your benefits, address specific concerns that may have come up in the interview, demonstrate your interest in the company and display your professionalism.

Thank you notes come in a variety of forms. They can be emails, letters, faxes or handwritten cards. The most important thing to remember about a thank you note is that to be effective, it must have substance. The following thank you notes were written after interviews. Compare them and consider who you would call back if you had a position to fill.

> **Letter #1:** Thank you for taking the time to meet with me yesterday. It was a pleasure to learn more about the company and your department. It sounds like it would be a great place to work. Please keep me in mind if an appropriate position should open in the future.

> **Letter #2:** Thank you for taking the time to meet with me yesterday. I especially appreciated your willingness to give me a warehouse tour. I was impressed with the cleanliness of your facility and I'm very familiar with the material moving equipment you are using. You can be assured I will require very little training. I look forward to joining your team AND your company softball league. I know I can hit a home run in both.

Letter #1, although polite, is unmemorable. The second letter not only displays courtesy to the manager for offering a plant tour, but also highlights the author's strengths and a non-work-related mutual interest (softball), which will make the candidate more memorable.

Getting a job today is all about standing out. Writing an influential thank you note is another opportunity to separate yourself from the crowd.

Making A Skills Portfolio

The skills portfolio is a visual aid that represents your work experience. It is a physical document you can share with the employer during an interview. It can be as simple as using a three-ring binder with plastic sleeves that hold your paperwork. I recommend dividing your skills portfolio into three sections: Credentials, Work Samples and Testimonials.

Credentials: Include your resume, diplomas, certificates of completion, a copy of your Social Security card, driver's license and any other documentation that is required for the job. Some people also include a "mission statement" or their commercial as a way of making their portfolios more personal.

Work Samples: Most people don't have or keep samples of their work, but if you can find pictures from the Internet of old work sites, logos from past employers or photos of you performing work, be sure to include them. These visuals will help jump-start the conversation about the work you have done and relax both you and the interviewer. Other work samples to include are reports and work documents you have written, flyers or safety posters you made or photos of things you have built, painted or repaired.

Testimonials: These are awards you have won, letters of recommendation, thank you cards and emails and other "atta boys." Be sure to save these in a file folder so you have them when you need them. And remember, never leave your skills portfolio behind. Ask the employer to make a photocopy or offer to send a copy of any document the employer would like to keep.

The skills portfolio isn't a necessity, but it is nice to have -- the icing on the cake. It will make your interview a memorable one and distinguish you from your competition.

Quick Tip:

"The most difficult part of getting to the top of the ladder is getting through the crowd at the bottom." -- Arch Ward

True Story:

During one of my rants on writing thank you notes, Joshua raised his hand and asked, "I interviewed with Pepsi Cola for a warehouse job two weeks ago. Is it too late to send a thank you note?" I told Joshua it is best to send your thank you note within 24-hours of the interview, but it is never too late to thank someone for their time. After class, Joshua approached me with a thank you note he had written in pencil on lined notebook paper. He had me correct the spelling and grammar. Then he hand delivered the note to the hiring manager he interviewed with two weeks earlier. The next day during class, Joshua's mother appeared at the door to deliver her son a message. Pepsi Cola had just called and offered Joshua a job. Was this a coincidence or did Joshua's thank you note make a difference? You decide.

CHAPTER V
RULES FOR DEVELOPING YOUR GAME (MARKETING) PLAN

The typical job hunter spends hours aimlessly wandering online job boards looking for job openings. This is one way to go about a job search, but it isn't very strategic. For one thing, a large percentage of the listings posted online are not viable jobs. They are often outdated postings, staffing agencies collecting resumes or multilevel marketing schemes. Second, by responding to advertised job openings, you are competing with hundreds of other job hunters who are sitting at home, just like you, applying for jobs in their pajamas. Your chances of getting a job from an online posting are a long shot.

If you want a more efficient and effective approach to looking for a job, begin by preparing a marketing plan. Anybody in advertising will tell you, if you are going to promote a product or service, you need a marketing plan. Selling your services in the job market is no different. Your marketing plan is a written document, a road map that drives your job search. In this chapter you will learn how to develop a marketing plan that includes the following components:

- Clarifying your career goal -- service you are selling
- Creating key messages -- benefits the employer will derive from hiring you
- Identifying target audiences -- potential employers who will want your services
- Selecting your strategies -- activities you will use to hit your targets
- Organizing your job-finding activities -- daily schedule to keep you motivated and on task

Clarifying Your Career Goal

Your career goal is the profession or trade you want to focus on. If you aren't sure of your goal or have several directions you could take, that is okay. Just remember, you will need a marketing plan for each one. For starters, list one career or job title you are thinking about here.

Career Goals_____

Creating Key Messages

This is your commercial -- the benefits you are selling. It should include the most important points you want to impress upon potential employers, such as relevant training and experience, hard and soft skills of the profession and required certifications and licenses. If there are unique reasons why you would be good in this position, be sure to include these key messages in your commercial. List five reasons why you would be good at the job you listed. These are your key messages.

1. _____
2. _____
3. _____
4. _____
5. _____

Identifying Target Audience (potential employers)

Instead of thinking "Who has a job opening?," you should be thinking, "Who could I potentially work for?" By getting to know employers before there are openings, you have a better chance of being considered and will reduce your competition. If an employer has met job candidates before a position becomes vacant, he knows he has several viable options to pick from. When it is time to fill a position, he may decide not to advertise the job, but rather select one of those candidates "on the bench." This practice is often referred to as "The Hidden Job Market." These are jobs you won't find advertised to the general public.

What kind of employer do you want to work for? Before you begin developing your target audience or potential employer list, think about your criteria for selecting an employer. What is important to you? Some suggestions are:

- **Size.** How big a company do you want to work for?
- **Location.** Can you get there by bus if you don't have a car? How long are you willing to commute?
- **Employment policy.** Has this company hired ex-offenders in the past?
- **Reputation.** What is its reputation for safety, salary, advancement?

List the criteria that are important to you when thinking about choosing an employer.

1. _____

2. _____

3. _____

How do you find these employers? The most efficient way to build your target list is by industry. For example, if you are considering warehouse work, you could group your targets by grocery, electronics and furniture warehouses. Then make a list of employers under each category. If a job in customer service is your objective, you might categorize your targets this way: retail clothing stores, telecommunications companies and hotels/motels. By grouping your targets, you can use similar resumes and cover letters without making major adjustments. Strive for 40 - 60 targets, or at least 20 in each category. You'll need more in a tough economy.

Where do you find these targets? Start with a phone book for your geographic location. If you don't get a phone book delivered to your home, you can find one in the local library. You can also use your favorite Web browser to search online. Other resources to help you develop your lists include:

- Business section of newspapers and business journals
- Trade unions and professional associations
- Chambers of commerce -- online and print directories
- Classified job postings and online job boards
- Online databases like www.hoovers.com and www.referenceUSA.com
- Your state's one-stop career center www.careeronestop.org
- People – talk with others/network

EXERCISE

Identify three industries you would like to work in based on the career or job title you chose. List the employers in each industry that you could potentially work for.

Industry 1:	Industry 2:	Industry 3:

Selecting Your Strategies

Once you have built your list, you will want to prioritize your targets into A, B and C groups, with the A group including your first-choice employers. How you prioritize your targets will depend on how they match up with the criteria you have specified. Each group will require a different set of strategies. You will want to do in-depth research on your A group of targets, find company contacts and monitor their Web sites. You may decide to do a mass mailing of your resume to the C group, as you won't want to spend as much time with companies in your third-choice group. Below is a list of common job search strategies. They are listed in their order of effectiveness.

Networking

Networking remains by far the most effective way of finding employment, particularly when the job market is tight. Just think about how you got your jobs in the past. If you found them through friends, relatives, former bosses or co-workers, then you got those jobs by networking.

Networking is establishing relationships with people you know and people they know, so that you can gather information, support and ideas. Your first generation network should include people with whom you are comfortable and have established relationships. They will refer you to a second generation of networking opportunities -- the people they know.

First Generation Network	*Second & Third Generation Networks*
Family	Anyone with information on your targets
Friends	Company "insiders"
Current/past co-workers and bosses	Hiring managers
Instructors and classmates	Human resources staff
Neighbors	Board members
Service people (doctor, hairdresser)	People of influence
Religious community	
Other volunteers	
Club/team members	
Case workers & parole officers	

Networking with your first generation group is easy. You can practice your commercial, share your marketing plan and discuss your concerns in a relaxed and informal manner. But when your first generation people introduce you to their networks of contacts, it can become more dicey, especially if you are the shy type. Developing phone scripts, preparing questions and having a marketing plan in place will make your meetings focused and purposeful. After you have had a few networking conversations, you will discover how easy and informative they can be.

Valuable networking conversations can happen almost anywhere -- on the bus, at your kids' soccer games, in line at the grocery store. Always have your business cards handy and your commercial rehearsed. Below are the 10 most popular and effective places to network if you are looking for employment.

Quick Tip

When you are networking with people you don't know well, don't ask about job openings. It makes people uncomfortable if they can't help you or don't want to reveal an opening they know about. Instead, ask your contacts if they have information about the companies you have targeted. They are more likely to be able -- and willing -- to help you with pertinent information that will help you to uncover vacancies and company contacts.

- Trade unions and professional association meetings
- Volunteer assignments -- ongoing
- One-time volunteer assignment, i.e., charity event
- Faith-based activities
- Golf courses, tennis courts and workout facilities
- Chamber of commerce meetings/events
- Community service organizations (Kiwanis, Rotary, Lions clubs)
- Political campaigns and social causes
- School, workshops, seminars
- Hobby clubs and support groups

Once you have identified someone you would like to talk to, take it upon yourself to set up a networking meeting. Having a phone script in front of you will make it easier for you to make the call. Be sure to do the following:

- Greet the person who answers the phone
- Give a brief version of your commercial (10-15 seconds)
- Be specific in what you are asking for
- Be mindful of your tone of voice -- be energetic and friendly

- Take notes during your conversation
- Follow up with a thank you note

 *EXAMPLE*

Sample phone script requesting a networking/information meeting:

"Hello, my name is Charles Floyd. Your neighbor, George Kelly, suggested I get in touch with you. He said you are an expert in the transportation industry, an area in which I want to work. I know you may not have an open position at this time, but I am interested in learning about your company and finding out if it is a good fit should an opening come up. Can you give me 20 minutes of your time for an information meeting? What is a convenient time for me to stop by?"

Random inquiry:

Hi, my name is _____. I would like to inquire about any current job openings you may have in (your field) _____.
My experience includes _____
_____.
I will be in the neighborhood tomorrow and would like to stop by and drop off my resume. What might be a good time for me to do that?

Specific job posting:

Hi, my name is _____. I am calling about the position you have posted for _____.
My experience includes _____
_____.
Could I set up a time to talk with you to discuss this position in more detail?

Don't be discouraged if the person you are contacting avoids you, doesn't want to meet you or refers you to the company Web site. Not everyone is inclined to participate in an information or networking meeting, but you will be surprised how many "strangers" will agree to meet with you.

Social networking

Don't overlook this valuable resource. Social networking is a great way to locate decision-makers, find job leads and connect with strangers who may have information that could be valuable to your job search. Two popular social media networks are Facebook and LinkedIn. Consider Facebook your den and LinkedIn your office. The former is more informal and the latter is professional. I recommend opening a free account with LinkedIn at www.linkedin.com. Fill out the profile using the information from your commercial and resume. Avoid using dates older than 10 years. It is up to you if you want to include a photo, but if you do, make sure it is professional looking. Many recruiters read LinkedIn profiles before they call job candidates for interviews. They also like to look at the recommendations. Ask three or four of the people you most trust to provide you

Quick Tip:
If you are meeting with a second or third generation contact, have questions prepared prior to your meeting. Ask questions about the industry, the company and the individual's career path. Your questions will keep the conversation moving and generate valuable information for your job search. See Appendix B for sample information meeting questions.

with recommendations on your LinkedIn account. Then begin inviting people from your first generation network to connect with you. If you have a special interest, such as cycling, golden retrievers, chess or renewable energy, join a LinkedIn discussion group. It is a great way to expand your network, which for most ex-offenders is pretty limited. You will make a cadre of friends who just might be able to help you with information to advance your job search.

Walking in

True Story:

One of my professional clients, Janice, was skeptical about networking. She preferred the traditional approach to job finding by looking for job postings on the Internet. One weekend while attending an air show, Janice struck up a conversation with one of the volunteers who was serving hot dogs. After reciting her commercial, she learned the volunteer was an attorney who had a need for someone with her qualifications. On Monday, she sent him her resume, and within two weeks Janice was happily employed by "the hot dog man."

Walking in and introducing yourself to an employer you have targeted can be a remarkably effective way to get a job. It is a variation on networking in that you are establishing a relationship and showing a sincere interest in a particular company. Early in my career, I got my first teaching jobs this way. Upon graduation, I made a list of the schools within the geographic area in which I wanted to work. On my days off from cashiering at K-Mart, I would dress up and, with resumes in hand, I visited each school on my list. Some principals refused to meet with me. Others pointed me to the human resources office. But a few kind souls took the time to chat with me, and a couple even gave me tours of their schools. As the new academic year approached, I was called by one of those principals to substitute teach. Within a week, I had a job offer.

Another example of "walking in" happened when I was the new marketing director at a local hospital. One fellow showed up every few weeks to chat with my secretary and find out if I was hiring. When I was ready to fill a vacancy, my secretary and other hospital staff were quick to recommend this individual, who eventually got the job. He had made his interest in working in the marketing department known without being pesky and had developed relationships with employees at the hospital who advocated for him. This strategy is called "surrounding the hiring manager," and it works.

Quick Tip:

"Persistence is what makes the impossible possible, the possible likely, and the likely definite."
-- Robert Half

As an ex-offender, it is particularly important that employers get to know you and like you. By walking in, you have a chance to meet people face-to-face and make a favorable impression before you fill out the job application or discuss your past record. Several students have told me that they got hired on construction projects by showing up early at a job site with their tools in hand, ready to work.

They may have been turned away a couple of times, but inevitably one of the regular workers would fail to show up and the foreman would need the extra help.

Online job boards and classified ads

Although not as effective as networking, responding to job postings online or in print is fairly easy and can be done at your convenience. To get the best results from your efforts, follow these guidelines:

Quick Tip:

Always submit your resume in two different formats. Send it online if requested, but also fax or mail it to the contact you have identified. You can put at the top of your resumes the words "Second Submission." You want to get your resume into the hands of a real live human being. Most likely, he or she will pass it along to the appropriate hiring manager.

- Find the name of the hiring manager or someone who will pass your resume along to the appropriate decision-maker. You can find contact names by calling the company's information number, listening to the automated phone directory, doing an online search, using social media networks such as LinkedIn and Facebook or by asking someone you know who works at your target company.
- Reference the job in the first paragraph, using the exact job title and include a job number if one is given.
- Read the requirements and match your qualifications. Use as many key words as you can so your resume will be picked up if scanned by a computer.
- Proofread your cover letter and resume.
- Don't include salary information. If asked, respond with "salary negotiable."
- Don't mention areas where you aren't qualified; always promote your strengths, don't mention your weaknesses

Some job boards I am partial to are www.indeed.com, www.simplyhired.com and www.craigslist.com. The first two are Web browsers and will pick up jobs from a number of job boards, such as Monster and CareerBuilder. I like the fact that they pick up jobs within specific zip codes and list the dates the jobs were posted. Over the years, Craigslist has become more unreliable with its job postings and is vulnerable to job scams, but I still like the fact that it offers a section at the bottom of the page called Gigs, where you can find freelance work. Web sites you will also want to check out if you have a criminal record include:

- www.hard2hire.com
- www.hirenetwork.org
- www.thenextstep99.com
- www.goodwill.org (jobs and careers)

If you are inclined to post your resume on Web sites with the hope that a recruiter will see it, do so on the Web site of your target companies if they allow it or on industry-related job boards. For example, if you are looking for truck driving jobs, post your resume on www.bigrigs.com. If you are looking for a job in sales, post your resume on www.salesladder.com. By posting your resume on general job sites, such as Monster or Careerbuilder, you are susceptible to receiving a lot of junk mail in your inbox. It also makes sense that recruiters would use industry Web sites that are more targeted as opposed to sifting through resumes on general sites. You can find industry-specific Web sites by using your browser and typing in "job for (name your profession)."

Job fairs

Don't expect to get a job offer at a job fair, but do attend them. Most employers participate

True Story:

Amanda really wanted to work as a barista at Starbucks. When she heard about a local job fair, she checked to see if Starbucks would be represented. She dressed in khaki pants and a navy blue polo shirt like the Starbucks baristas wore at her favorite coffee shop. At the job fair, Amanda received a rare job fair interview by a Starbucks recruiter and was hired on the spot.

as a public relations gesture, and very little hiring, if any, actually takes place. However, job fairs provide a great opportunity to network and learn about companies. Treat the job fair as you would an interview by dressing appropriately, having business cards and resumes available and your commercial rehearsed.

You can usually find out in advance which employers will be attending the job fair. Booths of your target employers are the ones you want to visit first. When it is your turn to talk to the company representative, give a firm handshake, look the individual straight in the eye and recite a short version of your commercial. Offer your resume and business card. Ask for the recruiter's business card in return, so you can contact her in the future.

Don't be shy about talking to the other job seekers standing in line with you. It is possible they are not looking for the same type of work or in the same location, but, like you, they have been out in the job market gathering information and may know of someone in your particular profession who is hiring. Likewise, offer information that may be helpful to others. What goes around, comes around.

What is the best time to attend a job fair? Most attendees arrive well before the doors open, mistakenly thinking first come, first hired. Since most employers don't hire at job fairs, the early birds are generally long forgotten by mid-morning. I recommend arriving an hour or two before the job fair is scheduled to end. By then, the lines have thinned out, the recruiters are relaxed and will often spend more time talking with you. When they are back at their desks sifting through a pile of resumes, you are more likely to be top-of-mind than someone they met in the rush of the morning.

Employment agencies

Some employment or staffing agencies will not work with ex-offenders because of liability issues. However, there are many that do. Save yourself and the recruiter time by calling first to inquire if the agency finds employment for those with criminal records or ask other ex-offenders which agencies they have used. If the agency is willing to work with you, be sure it doesn't require a fee. Although it isn't illegal to charge the job applicant, most reputable agencies derive their fees from the employer, not the job candidate.

To be clear on what the agency can do for you, ask questions. Most place job candidates in permanent, temporary or temp-to-hire jobs. Perhaps you are attending school or have other commitments and don't need a permanent job. Temporary jobs allow you to make some money, keep your skills current and get to know employers while working on your own timetable. A temp-to-hire job means the employer wants to check you out first before committing to hire you. It is also a good opportunity for you to decide if this is an employer you want to work for. Limit your temp-to-hire commitment to no more than three months. If an employer wants to hire you, he will wait until the contract with the staffing agency has expired before making an offer. Although working with a staffing agency gets you in the door, you will make less money than working for the company directly. Three months is a good gauge to determine if you and the employer are compatible. Any longer just means less money in your pocket.

The following agencies have hired ex-offenders in the past or are willing to consider individuals who have maintained clean records for a certain length of time. Hiring policies also vary by location and owners.

- Labor Works www.laborworks.com
- Labor Systems Temporary Services www.laborsystems.com
- ManPower www.us.manpower.com
- Command Staffing www.commandonline.com
- Labor Ready www.laborready.com
- Link Staffing www.linkstaffing.com
- One-stop career center www.careeronestop.org

Mail campaigns

Mass mailing your resume is costly, labor intensive and generally provides a very low return on your investment. Like most direct mail pieces, a response rate of 1 percent to 2 percent is considered good. That mean you would have to send out 100 resumes to get one or two responses. However, if you enjoy doing research and you are a good writer, I recommend writing very personal cover letters to your A list and sending them with your resume to let targeted employers know of your interest in their companies and why you would be a good fit. If you have a mutual friend or contact, use his/her name (with permission) in the first paragraph. Now you are writing a networking letter, and these tend to have the highest return on investment, especially if you follow up with a phone call. You will find a networking cover letter example in Appendix B.

Freelance/self-employment/contract work

When I moved to Seattle in the 1980s, I was changing careers (from teacher to public relations specialist), had no local network, and unemployment was hovering around 10 percent. Although I didn't have much experience in my new field, I was able to do some volunteer work and pick up a few freelance projects that helped me build a skills portfolio, develop referral sources and establish a network in the industry. After a year of pick-up jobs, I convinced the manager of an international public relations agency to hire me as an intern for three months (at less than market rate). When my stint was over, the manager made me an offer for full-time employment. Finally, my new career was launched.

Being self-employed has its advantages. For one, rarely does a client do a background check. It also fills the gap from prison to employment on your resume. Freelancing allows you the freedom to work a variety of jobs on your terms and provides you with a legitimate reason to contact employers you have targeted. The downside is that it is hard to get a business off the ground if you don't have capital or marketing savvy. Fortunately, there many businesses that don't require a lot of overhead and there are free resources to assist you with marketing. Start with the Small Business Administration (SBA) at www.sba.gov. There are offices in every state. The SBA Web site has all the information and forms you will need to start your own business. But don't stop there. Be sure to make an appointment with a SCORE counselor. These counselors are retired business executives who volunteer for the SBA and serve as mentors to new entrepreneurs. Depending on where you live, you may work with a SCORE counselor in person, usually at a library, on the phone or --most typically -- online. You can find out more about SCORE and how to get invaluable (and free) business advice at the SBA Web site.

Now that you have all the parts in place, you are ready to begin your marketing plan(s). See the sample below and then begin a plan of your own. You will find additional examples and forms in Appendix B.

EXAMPLE
Sample Marketing Plan

Career goal: Delivery Driver

Key messages:

- CDL -- Class A; doubles endorsement
- Clean driving record -- no accidents
- Experienced driving solo/long haul

- Operate pallet jack; forklift certified
- Accurate documentation skills
- Personable, reliable, sound judgment

Criteria for targets:

- Willing to hire ex-offenders
- Pay at market rate (or above)
- No long haul, local delivery only

Target audiences:

Grocery/food delivery:	Furniture delivery:	Appliance delivery:
Safeway (A)	Levitz (A)	Sears (A)
Albertsons (A)	Macys (A)	N.W. Appliances (B)
QFC (A)	Dania (B)	Albert Lee (B)
Amazon Fresh (B)	IKEA (B)	Pete & Bonnie's (C)
Whole Foods (B)	Scan Design (B)	Apex Appliances (C)
Godfather's Pizza (C)	Sears (A)	Kitchen Aide (A)
Toni Maroni's (C)		Whirlpool (A)

Strategies:

A Targets	B Targets	C Targets
- Post resume on company Web sites - Check Web sites at least once a week for postings - Identify 2-3 people in each company to contact - Call and request an information meeting or walk in and hand deliver resume, business card, cover letter - Call company HR and identify staffing agencies used by target company - Attend networking event where targets will be represented, i.e., job fairs	- Post resume on company Web sites - Check Web sites once a week for postings - Try to find one key contact - Send general letter of interest w/resume - Look for networking opportunities	- Post resume on company Web sites - Check Web sites every two weeks - Send general letter of interest along with resume

Organizing Your Job-finding Activities

Finding a job is a full-time job. You should be devoting at least 30 hours per week to job-finding activities if you are serious about obtaining employment. To keep your momentum going, it is helpful to establish a routine with daily and weekly goals. Keep a log and set goals for yourself at the beginning of each week. At the end of the week, evaluate how you did. If you are a morning person, you may want to do your phone calling first and save the research and writing for later in the day. Pace yourself and take breaks as needed. Don't beat yourself up if you didn't meet your weekly goals; resolve to try harder next week. And be sure to celebrate the small victories by doing something you enjoy such as a walk in the park, a call to a friend or time out to play with your kids.

Quick Tip:

Make an electronic or paper file for each company you have contacted. Record the information on whom you contacted and the type of interaction you had, i.e., online application, walked in a resume, attended company job fair, and when you intend to contact the company next. The job application, resume, cover letter and any other correspondence you have had with the company should be kept together for quick reference. A sloppy or disorganized job search can result in missed opportunities and embarrassing mistakes.

 EXAMPLE

Weekly Activity Log

Week of:

Activity – Weekly goal	Mon.	Tues.	Wed.	Thurs.	Fri.	Total
Research "A" targets -- send cover letter and resume -- 5						
Walk in resumes to "A" targets -- 5						
Send general cover letter and resume to "B" and "C" -- 10						
Monitor "A" job boards weekly -- 20						
Monitor "B" and "C" job boards -- 20						
Respond to ads and job postings -- 10						
Call to set up information meeting -- 1 - 2						
Contact or reconnect w/ staffing agency -- 1-2						
Attend networking event or meeting -- 1 - 2						

True Story

When Virginia was released from prison, she began attending job fairs. At one fair she had a lengthy conversation with a recruiter from a large grocery chain. She explained her circumstances and desire to have a fresh start. She continued to keep in touch with the recruiter with his permission. After a period of six weeks, the recruiter invited her in for an interview. Virginia answered many questions about her conviction as well as her experience and interest in the company. She was invited back for a second round of interviews, and many of the previous questions were brought up again. Virginia knew there were still some skeptics on the hiring panel, but eventually her advocates won out and she was offered a job as a stocking clerk.

CHAPTER VI: RULES FOR GAME DAY

You've worked hard to develop your communication pieces, research your targets and launch a strategic job search to which you have devoted at least six hours of each day. Your efforts are soon rewarded as employers begin setting up interviews. Let the games begin. This chapter describes the activities and behaviors that should occur during the three phases of the job interview:

- Before the interview
- During the interview
- After the interview

Before the Interview

As an interview contender, what you do before the interview is crucial. You must engage in three critical activities to be at the top of your game: research, practice and prepare.

Research

About the company

One of the first questions you may get asked in an interview is, "What do you know about our company?" Don't let this question take you by surprise. Be sure to visit the company Web site before embarking on an interview. You want to know what products or services are associated with the company; something about its mission, owners or executives; and the markets it serves. If you have time, you may want to search for the company on your favorite browser to read recent news articles and find out what others are saying about it. Did it recently have a layoff? Is it embroiled in a lawsuit? Has it had safety violations? The negative news will not be advertised on the company Web site, but you want to know about it. An employer wants to hire people who have an interest in the company. If you come across as someone who is just looking for a job, the interviewer will not be impressed. By demonstrating that you have done your research on the company, you will be considered a serious candidate.

The salary and benefits

Of course you want to know about salary and benefits, but you don't want to have this conversation too early in the interview or you will appear more interested in the paycheck than the job. Instead, do some investigating ahead of time. By researching this information *before* the interview, you won't need to ask about salary, and you will be prepared to provide an informed response if the interviewer should ask you about your salary requirements. There are many ways to get salary information. Consult your trade or professional association, visit your state's one-stop career center or look at similar job titles on job boards such as www.indeed.com. These sources will often provide you with salary and benefit information in relation to your geographic location and level of experience. Better yet, ask a company "insider," a friend or acquaintance who works for the company, how the salary and benefits are in comparison to other companies in the industry. The following Web sites will also provide you with basic salary information free of charge: www.payscale.com and www.salaryexpert.com. By having this information before the interview, you can concentrate on the job responsibilities. A job candidate who is eager to ask about salary and benefits comes across as someone who is desperate for a job.

The interviewer

You don't want to look like a stalker, but knowing a little bit about the interviewer can help you make a personal connection. Ask at the time the appointment is set for the interviewer's name and job title. Then check out some of the social media sites or conduct an online search to find out more about the person who will be interviewing you. Perhaps she just got a promotion or won an award for which you can offer your congratulations. Maybe he went to the same school or shares a similar interest in race cars, orienteering or video gaming. Bring this up in the conversation. People like to work with people they feel they know or who have similar interests. Your game strategy is to bond with the interviewer and get him to like you. Doing your research will help.

Practice

Your commercial

You have already prepared a commercial, but you will want to revisit it prior to the interview and tailor it to the job for which you are being interviewed. Re-read the job description carefully and weave the employer's key words into your commercial along with other attributes and experience you want to advertise. If the job description emphasized that the company is looking for someone with experience in Microsoft Excel and customer service, you will want to mention your expertise with Excel and customer service in your commercial. Practice saying your commercial, but don't memorize it. You want it to sound natural, not rehearsed.

Quick tip:

The order of your interview can influence your odds of getting hired. Candidates who are interviewed toward the end of the process have a better chance of getting an offer than those interviewed at the beginning.

Your stories

Behavioral or situational interviewing is a popular technique for interviewing job candidates. Employers want to know how you will respond in a given situation by asking for examples. They believe how you handled a situation in the past is a good indication of how you will behave in the future. Behavioral questions often begin with "Tell me about a time when ...." or "Give an example of how you ..."

In other words, employers are looking for stories. The best way to prepare for an interview is to write out six to 10 stories. These stories should be about how you made or saved money for an employer, fixed a problem, improved a process or quality, resolved conflict, helped your team members and took initiative. Review the stories you created in Chapter IV and add on to them. Don't hesitate to include stories from work you did in prison ... although you may want to leave out the location. The story is still valid. Practice telling your stories without using your notes. Use the B.A.R. format (Background, Action, Results) to keep your story concise and prevent the tendency to ramble.

Answers to difficult questions

Why have you been out of work so long? Where do you hope to be with your career in five years? What is your biggest weakness? What kind of boss brings out the worst in you? This is just a sampling of the most frequently asked interview questions. Be prepared for them. There are many resources available to help you prepare for frequently asked interview questions, including those in Appendix B of this book.

To prepare for an interview, make a list of the questions you dread being asked. Those are the questions you need to practice. Keep the negative responses brief and try to bridge to the positive. Always end on a positive note. For example:

Q. What did you like least about your last boss?

A. My last boss was very demanding and yelled a lot. Although I didn't like it at the time, I now realize he had high expectations of us and got us to perform to our full potential. Our team was often recognized for the quality of its work.

Talking about your criminal record

If the question hasn't come up already, toward the end of the interview you are obliged to bring up your conviction. Think carefully how you will tell your story and pick your words carefully. Keep the details of your conviction brief and bridge quickly to what you learned from your experience and how you are rehabilitated. Perhaps you got your GED in prison, tutored other inmates, performed community service or attended various support groups. Be sure to bring up these activities and end on a positive note.

EXAMPLE OF SCRIPT

I have two things I need to tell you before we complete this interview. The first is that I may not pass the background check. Several years ago I hung around with a group of bad guys and made some poor choices. I drank too much and was convicted of assault after a fight in a bar. During my time at the correctional facility I took the opportunity to refocus my life. I earned my GED, took classes on improving my interpersonal relationships and faithfully attend AA meetings. I have been clean and sober for more than a year and have a new and very supportive group of friends. I even had a chance to tutor a few guys who couldn't speak English very well. The second thing you should know is that I really want to work for your company and am committed to doing whatever it takes to prove my worth and make a substantial contribution. I am hoping you will give me that chance.

Preparation

Documentation

In preparing for your interview, you will want to make sure you take along the appropriate paperwork. Depending on the materials you need, having your information organized in a binder with pockets will be helpful. Below is a checklist of documents you might need:

- Driver license

- Social Security card or work authorization

- Birth certificate

- Extra resumes

- Certifications

- Diplomas and/or school transcripts

- Work samples

- References

- Master application (with complete information to help you fill out a job application if you haven't already)

- Directions to the interview

Interview clothes and appearance

There is a reason why "Dress for Success" books are popular. Your appearance can make or break your chance of getting hired. Common wisdom suggests you dress a level or two better than you would on the job. For example, if you are applying for a construction job, dress like you are ready to go to work. Make sure your shirt and jeans are clean (no rips, stains or slogans) and you are wearing appropriate work shoes. If you are applying for an office job, a sport jacket or sweater and tie

Quick tip:

Don't forget to take along the company phone number. In the unfortunate event that you are caught behind a traffic accident, have a flat tire or your bus breaks down, you can call ahead and give the interviewer a "heads up." It's not an auspicious beginning, but having courteously called ahead, there is a chance to redeem yourself.

for men demonstrate professionalism. For women, a pant suit or slacks and sweater ensemble (stay away from bold colors and suggestive necklines) will work in most situations. Avoid fragrances and jewelry that will distract the interviewer. A fresh haircut and good hygiene will work wonders. Don't wait until the day of your meeting to pick your interview attire. Inspect your clothes the night before for frayed cuffs, forgotten stains and missing buttons. Select clothes you like and make you feel good to add a little confidence boost. I have had some job

True story:

While working as the marketing director at a local hospital, it was my job to interview and hire the public relations staff. I clearly remember one job candidate who had a haircut that rivaled Bart Simpson's. I spent most of the interview pondering his hair rather than what came out of his mouth. Needless to say, he did not get the job, nor did I have the heart to tell him why.

candidates tell me they visit the job site prior to the interview to see what employees are wearing and then dress accordingly.

Notes

Most people assume notes are not allowed in an interview. Why not? Having a few notes in front of you will calm your nerves and suggests to the interviewer that you take the meeting seriously and have come prepared. Several human resources professionals I surveyed confirmed that bringing notes to an interview is OK. I suggest using an 8"x11" notepad or binder. On the top page include the following notes:

- Bullet points for your commercial. Don't write out the whole thing, but jot down the four or five key points you absolutely don't want to forget.

- Names of your stories. If you did the story writing exercise in Chapter II, you were asked to give each story a brief name. Make the name descriptive. "Angry Customer" may be too general to jog your memory. "Angry Bow Tie Man" will aid your recall.

- Questions to ask. The questions you ask are just as important as the questions asked of you. Prepare six to eight thoughtful questions that show your genuine interest in the company and position for which you are interviewing. Employers are impressed by job candidates who ask good questions. A list of suggested questions is offered in Appendix B.

Additional tips

- Arrive about 10 minutes ahead of your appointment. Any earlier and you look too eager; fewer than 10 minutes and you'll feel rushed.

- Make sure you get complete directions from the appointment setter. The interview may not be at the worksite, and you don't want to show up at the wrong place. A practice run the day before may be helpful.

- Try to get a good night's sleep and eat breakfast. You want to be at your best.

- Don't smoke or drink coffee before your interview; don't go into the interview chewing on gum or breath mints.

- Turn off your cell phone before walking into the meeting.

During the Interview

If you have researched, practiced and prepared for your interview as suggested at the beginning of this chapter, you will have the confidence and wherewithal to respond to almost any question that comes your way. So relax and enjoy the meeting. Remember, you are interviewing the company as well. Put your best self forward, while remaining genuine and enthusiastic. Here is a checklist of things you will want to remember during your meeting:

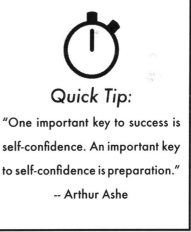

Quick Tip:

"One important key to success is self-confidence. An important key to self-confidence is preparation."

-- Arthur Ashe

- Pay attention to body language and eye contact -- don't slouch or fidget; lean forward and look the interviewer in the eye while speaking, although avoid a piercing stare.

- Wait for the interviewer to extend a handshake; make sure you offer a firm one without crushing any knuckles.

- Begin the conversation by commenting on something not work-related, perhaps the weather, a local sports team or something in the office that has caught your eye. If appropriate, now is a good time to use that bit of information you discovered about the interviewer in your research. If she recently received an award or promotion, be sure to extend your congratulations. You want to establish a rapport with the interviewer so you will be more memorable.

- Request a business card. It is best to do this at the beginning so you don't forget, but asking at the end of the interview also works. You want to make sure you have the interviewer's job title, contact information and the correct spelling of her name so you can follow up or ask additional questions if needed.

- Be sure to share a variation of your commercial at least two times. Repetition is good in an interview.

- Ask for permission to ask questions early on. Many interviewers will want you to wait until the end of the meeting, but by asking questions at the beginning you have a greater chance of establishing a dialog than with the traditional question/answer format.

- Ask for the job. Many interviewees are reluctant to do this, but if you have ever been in sales you know that the best way to close a deal is to ask for objections. The question can be stated in a couple of different ways: "Is there any reason why you wouldn't hire me for this position?" or "From what you have heard so far, how do you feel about my prospects for this job?" It is better to know right away that you don't have a particular skill or your conviction is the reason for not getting hired. It saves a lot of time waiting for the phone to ring.

- At the end of the interview, be sure to ask about next steps in the hiring process and when you can expect to hear from the company. Ask if you may contact the interviewer if you don't hear by the scheduled date or if you have additional questions. You want to leave the door open to reconnect with the interviewer and keep your name top of mind.

After the Interview

The interview may be over, but your work with this employer is not finished. There are three steps you need to take before you move on.

Critique yourself

How did you do? What did you do well? What do you need to work on? Here is a checklist to help you evaluate your interview performance:

- Presented a professional appearance
- Offered a firm handshake
- Maintained good eye contact
- Showed good posture and use of hand gestures
- Showed enthusiasm and confidence (smiled, projected voice)
- Established rapport (used ice breakers)
- Asked questions (showed interest)
- Created a dialog
- Avoided "umm, uh, like"
- Offered commercial 2x
- Told stories using B.A.R. format
- Avoided discussions about salary
- Made it clear you are interested in the job
- Asked for objections
- Asked about next steps
- Asked for business card

Write a persuasive thank you note

The art of writing an influential thank you note is discussed in detail in Chapter IV. Think back to your conversation with the interviewer and try to link a significant point in your conversation to your thank you note. If you told a powerful story or the interviewer repeatedly asked a specific question, be sure to refer to it in your follow-up, whether it is an email or written correspondence.

Apply for another job

Don't wait for the phone to ring with a job offer. Turn right around and apply for another job. No matter how certain you are that you "got the job," there are unforeseen circumstances beyond your control that could get in the way of a job offer. Perhaps the employer decided not to fill the job after all. Although your conviction was not an issue with the hiring manager, it could have been a deterrent for others involved in the hiring process. Maybe there was a hiring freeze or the job requirements changed and you no longer met the qualifications for the position. By applying for another job immediately after the interview, you won't feel you have lost ground if the job falls through.

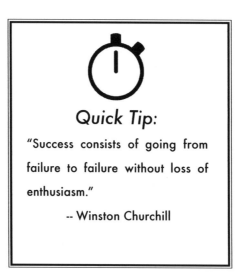

Quick Tip:

"Success consists of going from failure to failure without loss of enthusiasm."

-- Winston Churchill

CHAPTER VII: RULES FOR SCORING A WIN

This is the moment you have been waiting for -- the job offer. This chapter covers:

- Accepting the offer
- The art of negotiating salary and benefits
- Successfully transitioning into your new job

Accepting the Offer

After an arduous job search, it is tempting to accept a job offer on the spot. Unless there are a lot of other people in line as qualified as you are to do the job, it may not be the wisest move to immediately accept the offer. Once a job offer has been made, you have a small window of opportunity where you have some power to negotiate the terms of your employment. If the employer has spent a lot of time and money to find someone who is a good fit, he is not going to rescind the offer if you don't accept it immediately. First, you will want to thank the employer for the offer and let him know how excited you are about working for the company. (This implies you will be accepting the job.) Next you will want to ask for the offer in writing, so you can review the entire package. (This suggests good business sense.) Your script might sound something like this: "Thank you so much for the offer. I am very excited about working for your company. Before I start, I would like to see the job offer in writing and will get back to you the next day. Does that work for you?"

If the company cannot or will not give you the offer in writing, ask for someone to go over the benefits with you while you write them down. Tell the hiring manager you would like to review the terms of employment and will get back to him within 24 hours.

This gives you an opportunity to determine if there are any unexpected terms or conditions to the job you were not aware of, such as a noncompete clause or hidden expenses like the cost of parking or health care contributions. It also gives you an opportunity to determine what you may or may not want to focus on should you decide to negotiate for a better offer. Asking to review a job offer is not an unreasonable request. After all, your employer would not want you making financial decisions on behalf of the company without careful consideration. Depending on your situation, you will have to decide the downside to not accepting the job instantly.

THE A.R.T. of Negotiating Salary and Benefits

Most ex-offenders are so eager to get back to work, they are afraid to negotiate salary and benefits, fearing the employer will retract the offer if they appear less than thrilled with the compensation. It is true that in a lackluster economy, the employee doesn't have a great deal of leverage to negotiate compensation, and an ex-offender may have even less. However, by the time the employer has made an offer, he has invested a great deal of time and money in the job search process and is often expecting to entertain a counter offer if it is reasonable and done in a professional manner. The employer knows that if he starts out with an unhappy employee, he will be searching for a replacement before too long.

Negotiating your salary for a new job can be an emotional issue. When it comes to attaching a dollar amount to your worth, it is difficult to separate ego from the marketplace. But it doesn't have to be that way if you do your research and take a strategic approach to negotiating compensation. The strategy works like this:

Avoid the subject

Reverse the question

Tell a range.

Avoid the subject

During the interview, when asked about your salary requirement, a simple response such as, "My requirements are flexible," or "My salary is negotiable," may be enough to move the conversation along. However, most interviewers will push a little harder for a response. You may explain that it is difficult to answer the salary question until you know more about the scope of the job and the responsibilities involved. If you are asked specifically how much you made in your last job, point out that the salary you made in your previous position isn't applicable to the one for which you are interviewing, or respond by saying, "I made market rate for my last job." (After all, no one wants to reveal that she made $.42/hour working in the prison kitchen.)

Reverse the question

Many interviewers will continue to probe for an answer to the salary question. Don't take the bait. Your next course of action is to get the employer to state a number. Respond by asking, "What is the range you normally pay for this position?" or "Based on what you know of my experience, what do you consider my qualifications to be worth?" If the interviewer does offer a range, conceal your joy or dismay and simply acknowledge that the range is "within the ballpark." If the range is higher than you expected, you don't want to appear too eager. If it is lower, there may be aspects of the job or benefits that you can negotiate to make the compensation package work for you. Do your research and know what you're worth in the market. This way, you will know if the employer's first offer is a lowball or fair and well thought out.

Tell a range

In some cases you may be forced to mention a salary figure first. This is where researching wages prior to an interview will pay off. With the wealth of knowledge floating through cyberspace, there is no excuse for not knowing what you are worth in the marketplace for a specific job. A few good online resources are www.payscale.com, www.indeed.com and www.salary.com. They give you national, regional and local comparisons. Many professional and trade associations conduct a salary survey every year or two among their members and should be consulted as a part of your research. Better yet, call the company's human resources department and ask for the salary range of the job that you are considering. Many will give you that information up front. By talking to current and former employees, you will also find out whether the company's salary and benefits are above, at or below market rate.

As you think about the job and how you want to be compensated, have three price points in mind: The lowest you will accept, the market rate and 10 to 15 percent above market rate. Then start your negotiations by asking for the top of your range.

It's not all about money

Your salary is important, but it shouldn't be the only consideration for accepting or declining a job offer. Take into account the total compensation package.

There are many other benefits to consider. Will the employer supply your tools and personal protective equipment? Does the company pay for re-certifications and additional training that will enhance your ability to do your job and make you more marketable? What kind of opportunities for advancement does the company offer? Will it pay your cell phone bills and/or commuting expenses? If you are covered under your spouse's or partner's medical plan, some employers will allow you to waive your medical benefits and increase your base salary. Others will be willing to negotiate vacation days or shift hours. Most important, consider the job itself and the career potential. Having a job that gives you great satisfaction may be worth more than any employer can afford to pay. Here is how a conversation about salary might play out:

EXAMPLE #1

Employer: Thomas, we are excited about making you an offer. We need a good carpenter like you for our company and can offer you $15/hour. When can you start?

Thomas: That's terrific. I am excited about working for your company. You won't be sorry that you hired me, and I can start tomorrow if you want. But first I would like a few more details about your offer. Do you have something in writing I can look at?

Employer: Listen Thomas, we're a small company. After three months, we offer basic medical at an employee contribution of $50 per pay period, five paid holidays and two personal days. After one year with our company, you'll get $200 to apply to any kind of additional training you might want.

Thomas: That sounds fair. It's just that the salary seems a little low. Based on my research and similar jobs I've looked at, in this city non-union carpenters with my experience are making in the range of $16 - $20/hour. Would you consider a middle range of $18 and throw in new shoes and a tool belt?

Employer: Well we didn't really budget the position for that amount. I can give you money for new shoes and a tool belt. Perhaps I can go as high as $16.

Thomas: I really appreciate your helping with the shoes and tool belt, but the wage is still a bit below market. What do you think about $16.50 with a bump to $17 after three months? You won't regret a penny of it. I'll write up a letter of understanding for you to sign with those terms so you don't have to go to any trouble.

Employer: Thomas, if you are as good a carpenter as you are negotiator, then you're worth it. Go ahead and write up the letter. I'll see you tomorrow at 7 a.m. Here's an advance of $200 for those shoes and tool belt.

EXAMPLE #2

Employer: Irving, I am calling to make you a job offer. When can you start?

Irving: Great! I know you won't regret this. I am going to have to give my employer two weeks notice, but I think he will be willing to let me go early. Is there something in writing I can look at so I know what your total compensation package is?

Employer: Sure, I'll fax it over. Stop by after work tomorrow and you can fill out the rest of the paperwork.

Next day

Irving: Bob, I am really excited about working for your company. I had a chance to review your offer. The benefits look good, but the base salary seems a little low compared to the fair market rate. Would it be possible to bump it up by 10 percent?

Employer: Irving, I would love to give you more, and I think you are worth it. But I had a difficult time convincing my boss to add this position. I can't go back to him and ask for more money.

Irving: O.K., I totally understand. But I will be taking a slight cut in pay coming to work for you. What about a one-time signing bonus of $1,000? That would just about make up the difference and not impact my base salary.

Employer: No can do, Irving. I am just not in a position right now to offer you more money. I will understand if you can't take the job, but we would sure like to have you on the team.

Irving: I like your company and I know there are opportunities here for me in the future. Would you consider paying my cell phone bills since I will be using my own phone for work and for my re-certification expenses?

Employer: It is certainly something I can consider since phone expenses come out of a different budget. Let me talk to the owner and see if we can put you on our company calling plan and get back to you on that.

Transitioning into Your New Job

Congratulations! You're about to start your new job. You finally have the break you were looking for and you don't want to blow it. First impressions count and, unfortunately, we tend to judge others right away. The advice below is meant to help you look and act professionally from day one as you successfully transition into your new job.

Make your boss look good

One of the best things you can do is to make your boss or whoever hired you look good. When you shine, he shines. Here are a few tips to start.

Watch how your boss acts and what he likes. Is this person formal, friendly, a neat freak, a fitness buff? As much as you can, try to fit in with your boss's way of doing things and the corporate culture. Asking co-workers about the best way to work with the boss will give you valuable insights.

Shortly after starting work, have a conversation with your boss so you are absolutely sure you know what he expects of you. Keep him informed of what you are doing and any problems that arise. Ask for ways to improve your work.

Put thought into your appearance

Your first day on the job will set the tone with your co-workers, so the first impression they form of you is important. Nothing says more about you than how you dress. Find out in advance about the company dress code. Make sure your clothes are in good condition and fit well. Avoid T-shirts with controversial slogans or suggestive clothing that sends an unprofessional message. Take special care in your grooming. Is a haircut in order? Too much perfume or cologne? Do you have the right shoes for the job? Are your tools in good condition?

Quick tip:

When negotiating with an employer, use language such as "Would it be possible ... Could you consider ... It sounds less demanding and more respectful.

Be punctual and reliable

Being on time is the most basic measure of professionalism. When you are late, everyone notices. Be sure you know how long it will take to get to your new job and leave plenty of time to compensate for the unexpected, such as bad traffic or congested parking.

Even better than arriving and leaving on time is coming in early and staying late. Coming in 15 minutes early and sometimes being the last one to leave will add up favorably in the eyes of your boss.

Limit your Internet and cell phone use

Don't use the Internet for personal use. And never go to controversial sites. You could be fired on the spot. Avoid sending emails that contain jokes or off-colored remarks to co-workers or friends. If you get an email from a co-worker, answer it right away, either with a reply, a phone call or face-to-face contact with the sender.

Limit your cell phone use, especially for personal calls. Only make personal calls when you absolutely have to, and keep them short ... under a minute. Keep your cell phone on silent or vibrate. A ringing cell phone disturbs everyone around you. Even if you have a fun ringtone, it may not be appreciated by co-workers.

Be friendly ... Be professional

Treat every day like you are at a job interview. What you do and say on the job ultimately reflects on your employability and chance for promotions. Don't use profanity on the job. Avoid discussing your private life at work. Don't gossip about other employees or talk negatively about the company or other employers you may have worked for. Stay away from negative people. No matter how good things are, there are always people who see the downside. It is easy to get caught up in their negativity. You want to develop a reputation as one of those "positive people."

Finally, remember the Golden Rule: "Treat others the way you would like them to treat you." Be friendly to everyone, whether it is the president of the company, secretary or janitorial staff. Greet them all with a smile and "Good morning." "Please" and "Thank you" go a long way to giving the impression of politeness and respect.

Get to know your co-workers

One of your first tasks as a new employee should be to get to know everyone with whom you will be involved. Ask for and use your co-workers' names. Find out what they do. Learn the professional language or jargon that is specific to their business and positions. The administrative or support staff (human resources, accounting, clerical) are especially important to befriend because they know how to get things done and what resources are available. The maintenance staff and computer technicians will also be valuable resources in helping you do your job.

Take advantage of company training opportunities

Participate in any on-the-job training, certification programs or workshops the company offers. If you haven't been invited, ask your boss if you can attend. An employee who is continually working on his professional development and is cross-trained to perform multiple functions becomes a valuable asset to any employer. This also goes a long way to establishing job security.

Make an impact

Be willing to work extra hours or volunteer for jobs no one else wants. Gestures like these, especially during your probationary period, will not only establish your reputation as a hardworking and collaborative employee, but will also reassure the employer that he made the right decision in hiring you.

Volunteer your ideas

Don't be afraid to share the knowledge, skills, education and experiences that you have acquired in your journey through life. Be willing to allow your co-workers to learn from you. We often don't realize that our own experiences have a richness and value from which others can benefit.

Gather references and letters of recommendation

Save performance evaluations, letters of recommendation, perfect attendance and customer service awards and other "atta boys" you receive. They may not seem important to you now, but they could come in handy in the future as they are proof of good performance and teamwork.

As they say in the U.S. Army, "Be all you can be." Make your new job be all it can be as well. Take advantage of this opportunity to learn new skills, make valuable contacts and show what you can contribute. It is a second chance to create a new and meaningful life for yourself and those you care about.

EXERCISE

Now that you have learned to play the job-finding game, return to the last page of the introduction in this book. Re-test your Job-finding I.Q. You will be amazed at the improvement.

APPENDIX A: RESOURCES

Government Programs

Work Opportunity Tax Credit
U.S. Department of Labor - Employment & Training Administration
WTOC Fact Sheet
www.doleta.gov/business/Incentives/opptax

Federal Bonding Program
U.S. Department of Labor
www.bonds4jobs.com

One-Stop Career Centers
U.S. Department of Labor
www.careeronestop.org

National H.I.R.E. Network
Resources for ex-offenders by state
www.hirenetwork.org

U.S. Small Business Administration
To start your own business
www.sba.gov

Community Programs

The Salvation Army
Programs that help: Prisoner Rehabilitation
www.salvationarmyusa.org

Goodwill Industries International, Inc.
Who we serve: People with criminal backgrounds
www.goodwill.org

Volunteer Opportunities

Volunteers of America

Volunteer with our local offices

www.voa.org

United Way

Find your local United Way

www.unitedway.org

Volunteer Match

Find a place to volunteer

www.volunteermatch.org

General Job-finding Websites

www.rileyguide.com

www.jobhuntersbible.com

www.quintcareers.com

www.bls.gov/oco (Occupational Outlook Handbook)

www.careeradvisorsonline.com (See Career Resources)

Job Finding Books Specifically for Ex-offenders

The Ex-offender's Quick Job Hunting Guide, Ron Krannich, Ph.D., 2009

Best Jobs for Ex-offenders, Ron Krannich, Ph.D., 2009

The Ex-offenders' Job Interview Guide, Caryl and Ron Krannich, 2009

Jobs for Felons: How to find employment if you have a criminal record, Michael Ford, 2009

I Need A J-O-B: The ex-offenders job search manual, Louis Jones, 2005

Best Resumes & Letters for Ex-offenders, Wendy Enelow and Ron Krannich, 2006

APPENDIX B: MORE EXAMPLES

SAMPLE FUNCTIONAL/SKILLS RESUME

CHARLES FLOYD
1904 Arthur Street, Adairsville, GA 30103
229-221-1936 ~ charles.floyd@gmail.com

WAREHOUSE WORKER
Domestic and International ~ Ground, Air and Ocean

Dependable Warehouse Clerk with expertise in shipping and receiving. Self-starter with strong communication and problem-solving skills. Skilled at negotiating rates and discounts with freight companies to save money and reduce turn-around time. In excellent physical condition with ability to lift more than 50 lbs. Forklift certified. Relevant experience includes:

Shipping:
- Ship small parcels in compliance with UPS, FedEx and DHL requirements
- Prepare shipping documents and mailing labels quickly and accurately
- Handle freight estimates and claims; able to handle shipping problems with diplomacy
- Schedule daily pickups and load shipments when necessary

Receiving:
- Verify incoming shipments and invoices
- Record contents and condition of shipment, using scanners to record barcodes and enter information into computer
- Unload and route shipments to appropriate locations or deal with customers directly when picking up shipments

Equipment:
- Certified forklift operator with excellent safety record
- Operate reach truck, pallet jack and clamp truck

Employment History

Hammer The Handyman*	2010 - present
Self-employed	
State of Minnesota, Stillwater, MN**	2006 - 2010
Maintenance Worker	
Big Box, Inc., St. Michael, MN	2000 - 2005
Shipping/Receiving Clerk	

Education/Training

Forklift certification. Training in forklift safety, materials handling, and preparing material safety data sheets. Basic computer skills. High school graduate.

Notes: * Performed odd jobs while looking for work ** Period of incarceration

SAMPLE CHRONOLOGICAL RESUME

LESTER GILLIS
125 South Street, Chicago, IL 60302 ~ 312.193.1127 ~ lester.j.gillis@yahoo.com

---

GENERAL MAINTENANCE
Proactive ~ Good Follow-through ~ Customer-focused

Versatile Maintenance Worker with experience in construction and heavy cleaning. Demonstrate good manual dexterity and problem-solving skills. Recognized as a team player who will do whatever it takes to deliver the highest quality work within critical timeframes. Core competencies include:

- Perform general repairs to buildings, grounds and office areas
- Experienced in demolition/remodeling
- Demonstrate knowledge of carpentry, painting, drywall, mechanical repairs
- Operate heavy equipment/machinery, i.e., jackhammers, mixers, forklifts, pneumatics/power tools
- Communicate effectively oral/written

- Familiar with guidelines for safe working practices including handling of hazardous materials
- Read blueprints, schematics, manuals
- Operate/maintain maintenance equipment such as sanders, buffers, vacuums, pressure washers, sweepers
- Work collaboratively with a variety of trades and journeymen

RELEVANT EMPLOYMENT

Lead Technician, Bright Hood Cleaning Service, Chicago, IL (2009–2010)
- Supervised up to three employees completing 2 – 3 jobs per day.
- Cleaned kitchen appliances, exhaust fans, hood vents and external ducting.
- Accounted for and maintained company vehicle and work equipment.
- Resolved service issues and provided exceptional customer service.

Construction Worker, Brennan Construction, Skokie, IL (2006 – 2009)
- Worked on residential remodels, performing framing, drywall, concrete pouring, tile and countertop installations, foundation work and other jobs as required.
- Maintained a 100% accident-free safety record.
- Followed OSHA construction safety guidelines.
- Quick to learn new skills required on-the-job and trained others as required.

Cleaning Crew, State of Illinois, Decatur, IL (2000 – 2005)*
- Cleaned public areas such as dining halls and offices.
- Maintained floors; operated buffers.
- Handled and disposed of hazardous materials and cleaning agents.

OTHER EMPLOYMENT
Also worked as a telemarketer in Kansas and roustabout in the Texas oil fields.**

EDUCATION AND TRAINING
Received extensive on-the-job technical and safety training
High school diploma, Roosevelt High, Chicago, IL

Notes: * Period of incarceration ** Could be assumed these jobs are recent but not relevant to the job objective and performed during a gap in time

SAMPLE NETWORKING COVER LETTER

LESTER GILLIS
125 South Street, Chicago, IL 60302
312.193.1127 ~ lester.j.gillis@yahoo.com

November 4, 2011

Att: Hiring Manager, Thrifty Maintenance
Re: Maintenance Custodian #063

This is in response to your job posting for a Maintenance Custodian. Your foreman, Mack Greene*, thought I would be a good fit for this position and suggested I apply.

I know Thrifty Maintenance has an excellent reputation in the industry, so I was pleased to see you have an opening that is a good fit with my skills and experience. Attached is a resume. A summary of my relevant custodial qualifications includes:

- Experience cleaning and maintaining commercial and residential properties, including general structural repairs and remodeling work.

- 100% accident-free record and excellent knowledge of OSHA safety guidelines and hazmat regulations.

- Good manual dexterity and mechanical ability; can operate a forklift, backhoe, hand/power tools and other heavy equipment.

My employers have described me as easy going, a good problem solver and someone they can depend on to get the job done right. When I worked for Brennan Construction, I was able to get a time critical dry wall job done in one day, when it normally took two.** My past experience, ability to catch on quickly and work efficiently will be of benefit to your overall productivity and quality of service. I look forward to meeting you to discuss in more detail how I can contribute to the Thrifty Maintenance team.

Regards,

Lester Gillis

Notes:
* A networking letter uses the name of a mutual acquaintance and is effective in getting the employer's attention.

** Nice use of an example that shows the value the job candidate can contribute.

SAMPLE EMAIL REQUESTING AN INFORMATION/NETWORKING MEETING

To: theboss@blackburnindustries.com

Subject: Your company expansion*

Dear Mr. Blackburn:

I recently read that Blackburn Industries is opening a new plant in Lenexa, KS. As an experienced electronics assembler, I am writing to express my interest in working for your company. Although you may not have an opening now, I know you will at some point and I would like to discuss future opportunities at Blackburn Industries.** Attached is my resume. Highlights of my relevant qualifications include the following:

- Skilled troubleshooter and sharp observer; my ability to mitigate potential problems saved my former employer money and embarrassment by identifying and resolving incorrect wiring on an electronic component prior to delivery to the customer.

- Knowledgeable of lean manufacturing; in my last position I helped reorganize the assembly line which increased productivity by 15%.

- Skilled using hand, power and precision tools; possess excellent soldering skills and manual dexterity.

- Positive attitude; my co-workers say I am approachable and collaborative. I am always there for them.
- Extremely resourceful, flexible, and a diligent worker as former bosses and co-workers can attest.

I will call you next Monday to arrange for a mutually convenient time to meet.*** Thank you in advance for your consideration.

Sincerely,

Harry Longabaugh
harry.longabaugh@gmail.com
913.223.3456

Notes:
* Do not indicate you are looking for a job in the subject line. Make your subject relevant to the reader to ensure he will open it.

** It is a good idea to contact an employer prior to an open position to express your interest in working for the company.

*** If you say you are going to call to set up a meeting, be sure to follow-through.

SAMPLE HANDWRITTEN THANK YOU NOTE: WAREHOUSE WORK

Dear Ms. Plumber,

Thank you again for the opportunity to interview yesterday for the warehouse position at Big Box Warehouse. I appreciated the hospitality you and your staff showed me.

Based on our conversation, I am convinced my background and skills are a good fit with the job you described. My prior warehouse experience with Lumber Depot and the state of Minnesota and my ability to safely operate and repair a variety of moving equipment will result in increased productivity and cost savings for Big Box Warehouse. I look forward to hearing from you and becoming a member of your team.

Regards
Charles Floyd

SAMPLE THANK YOU EMAIL: GENERAL MAINTENANCE

Dear Grant,

Thank you for inviting me to interview for the custodial position at Thrifty Maintenance. I was impressed by your prestigious list of customers and state-of-the-art facilities.

I believe my general maintenance and custodial work in residential and commercial settings show my breadth of experience. My ability to get along with all types of people and fluency in Spanish make me a good fit for your culturally diverse work crew.

Working in a fast-paced, high productivity environment is where I thrive. I am eager to apply this energy and expertise to the Thrifty Maintenance team.

Sincerely,

Lester Gillis

SAMPLE MARKETING PLAN

Job objective: Retail Sales Associate

Key messages:

- Mechanical/automotive/electronic knowledge
- Persuasive communicator
- Good with people
- Resourceful finding leads
- Proven track record of closing sales
- Demonstrate good follow-through and problem solving capabilities
- Organized; pay attention to details

Criteria for targets:

- Within a 45 minute commute
- Room for advancement
- Hired ex-offenders in the past

Target audiences:

Auto/Auto supply:	Electronics:	Office Equipment:
Valley Toyota (A)	Best Buy (B)	Sears (C)
Southwest Pontiac (A)	Radio Shack (B)	Brownies Office Supplies (B)
Grady's Ford (A)	Frye's (B)	Office Depot (C)
Shucks (C)	Martin's Electronics (A)	Fred's Office Machines (A)
Big Boy Auto Supplies (B)	Stover's Electronics (A)	Boyd's Office Furnishings (B)
	N.W. Electronics (A)	

Strategies:

A Group	B Group	C Group
Research companies	Send resume & cover letter expressing interest	Send generic resume and cover letter expressing interest
Write customized resume and cover letters	Monitor Web site every two weeks for job postings	Monitor Web sites every two - three weeks
Hand deliver resumes and cover letter to manager	Find "insiders" to talk to	
Follow up every other week		
Monitor Web site postings once a week		
Find "insiders" to talk to		

SAMPLE FORM: MARKETING PLAN

Job objective:

Key messages:

-

-

-

-

-

Criteria for targets:

-

-

-

-

Target audiences:

Industry 1:	**Industry 2:**	**Industry 3:**

Strategies:

A Group	B Group	C Group

SAMPLE FORM: PRODUCTIVITY LOG

Weekly Activity Log

Week of:

Activity – Weekly goal	Mon.	Tues.	Wed.	Thurs.	Fri.	Total

Note: Suggested activities might include researching potential employers, walking-in to express interest in a company, sending a networking letter and resume, attending a networking event, meeting with a friend or connection, following-up on job leads, applying for jobs online, or contacting an employment agency.

SAFE QUESTIONS TO ASK IN AN INTERVIEW

About the company

What do you like about working for this company? What made you want to work here?

How would you describe the culture of this company?

What types of people seem to do well in this company?

How would you describe your company's safety record?

What are the challenges facing this company?

What kind of turnover rate does the company have?

How strongly does the organization try to promote from within?

How is your company doing financially?

About the job

Why is this position available?

Who would I report to?

What would a typical day in this job look like?

What would be my first assignment?

What are the challenges that have to be faced in this position?

What would you expect me to accomplish the first week, month on the job?

Are there any internal candidates for this job?

What do you think it takes to be successful in this job?

How will you know when you have found the right person for this job?

What about my resume made you decide to call me in?

About the work environment

What do you think is your company's greatest strength/weakness?

How does the company promote personal and professional growth?

How does the company recognize good performance?

Does the company support additional training? Can you give an example?

How would you describe your management style?

How would you describe the culture of your department? Of the company?

What does your company do to keep good workers?

How many hours a day/week do you typically work?

About the process

From what you know about me so far, do you think I would be a good fit for this job?

Are there any concerns you might have that would prevent you from hiring me for this position?

Is there anything else you need to know about me to make a decision to hire me?

When can I start?

What are the next steps in the hiring process?

When do you expect to make a decision?

When can I expect to hear from you?

May I call you if I have additional questions?

May I have your business card?

QUESTIONS FOR INFORMATION/NETWORKING MEETINGS

How long have you been working in this field?

What was your career path like?

What kind of education is required to do the kind of work you do?

What are the most important skills required for this kind of job?

What is the future outlook for this type of work?

What do you like about this particular company?

What kind of advice might you have for someone like me to break into the field/company?

Is there anyone else you suggest I talk to? May I use your name when contacting him?

FREQUENTLY ASKED INTERVIEW QUESTIONS

Selling personal strengths ...

Tell me about yourself.

What is your greatest strength?

What can you offer us that someone else can't?

Why should I hire you?

What are your most important accomplishments?

Describe the biggest mistake you have made in your career.

Tell about a career accomplishment that you are really proud of.

Overcoming Negatives and Objections ...

What is your greatest weakness? What do you need to work on?

Have you ever been fired or asked to resign?

Why did you leave your last job?

Why have you been out of work so long? What have you been doing?

What is the biggest mistake you have ever made? Tell about a time you failed.

Describe a time you had to deal with a difficult boss/co-worker/customer. How did you handle it?

What is the most significant criticism you have ever received from a boss?

What kind of boss brings out the worst in you?

Responding to questions about personal factors ...

What are your career goals?

What have you done to increase your personal development?

How do you feel about overtime?

Give an example of how you handle stress on the job.

Give an example of how you are a team player.

What are the things that motivate you?

How do you feel about your career progress? Where do you want to be in five years?

What qualities do you most admire in people?

Tell about a time you had to make an important decision on your own.

Describe the greatest challenge you have had in your career.

What is the most important lesson you have learned in your career?

We need someone who is resourceful. Describe a situation where you were resourceful.

What have you done that shows initiative? Give an example.

Talk about an effective method or procedure you have established or improved.

How do you handle difficult and demanding people? Give an example.

What are your salary requirements? What did you make in your last job?

Job factors...

Describe your perfect job. (This is the one!)

What is most important to you in a job?

Why do you want to change careers?

How long will it take before you make a positive contribution to our organization?

Describe a time you were criticized on your job.

What frustrates you about your job?

What is the worst thing you have heard about this organization?

What duties have you enjoyed the most? Least? Why?

What position do you expect to hold in five years?

Why would you like to work for us? What do you know about us?

What kind of supervisors do you like the most? Least? Why?

How have your supervisors helped you grow?

What did your last supervisor rate you highest and lowest in your last job?

What kind of supervisor gets the best results out of you?

Specifically for ex-offenders...

Why were you in prison? What was your crime?

How do I know you won't re-offend?

How do I know I can trust you?

What was it like in prison?

What is your current living situation?

How long do you plan to be around?

What have you learned from your prison experience?

Are you willing to start at the bottom?

Illegal questions...

How old are you?

Are you married?

Do you have a car?

How many children do you have? What are their ages? Do you plan on having more?

Have you ever been arrested? (It is legal to ask about convictions; not arrests.)

What is your religion/ethnic background/sexual preference?

Terry Pile, MS, GCDF

Terry Pile is a creative and versatile career counselor and coach specializing in helping people find and succeed in the work they love. She has been working with individuals and businesses nationwide since 2000.

Terry has a Master's degree in education from Indiana University and a certificate in career development facilitation from the University of Washington. She is certified by the Center for Credentialing and Education as a Global Career Development Facilitator (GCDF). Career counseling is Terry's third career. She taught in the public schools and was a marketing/public relations executive for Ogilvy & Mather, PR, and a medical center. Now she teaches individuals to market themselves for successful employment.

In addition, to consulting and training, Terry writes feature articles on career issues in the print and electronic media. She has published five electronic books on career topics through Get to the Point Books, www.gettothepointbooks.com. She is the co-author of *Changing Careers after 40: Real Stories, New Callings*. This is her second book.

To contact Terry, visit her Web site at www.careeradvisorsonline.com

Made in the USA
Middletown, DE
12 March 2016